REJOICING IN THE LORD

A STUDY OF THE BOOK OF PHILIPPIANS

DR. KARRY D. WESLEY

© 2001 by Karry D. Wesley. All rights reserved.

Printed in the United States of America.

Cover design by Imaginuity Interactive, LLC

Packaged by WinePress Publishing, PO Box 428, Enumclaw, WA 98022. The views expressed or implied in this work do not necessarily reflect those of WinePress Publishing. The author(s) is ultimately responsible for the design, content, and editorial accuracy of this work.

No part of this publication may be reproduced, stored in a retrieval system or transmitted in any way by any means, electronic, mechanical, photocopy, recording or otherwise, without the prior permission of the copyright holder except as provided by USA copyright law.

Unless otherwise noted all Scriptures are taken from the King James Version of the Bible.

ISBN 1-57921-387-1
Library of Congress Catalog Card Number: 2001089590

To my wife & sons:
Cheryl, Chris, Karl, and Charles.

To my friend, colleague, and mentor:
The Reverend O.C. Collins, Jr.
of Memphis, Tennessee.

To my father:
Henry Lee Wesley, Sr.

Contents

CHAPTER 1
The Family of Faith 7

CHAPTER 2
Addressing Adversity and the Adversary 23

CHAPTER 3
Living in the Lord 33

CHAPTER 4
I Am My Brother's Keeper! 44

CHAPTER 5
The Discipleship Program 60

CHAPTER 6
Ministers on the Mission Field 74

CHAPTER 7
Merited Favor:
When the Gains Outweigh the Losses 87

Chapter 8
Those Were Not the Good Old Days 104

Chapter 9
The Wheat and the Tares 112

Chapter 10
Dealing with Discord Among Disciples 123

Chapter 11
Don't Worry, Be Happy! 130

Chapter 12
Contentment in Christ 135

Chapter 1

The Family of Faith

Philippians 1:1–11

The Formation
    The Background of the City
    The Birth of the Church
    The Bonds of the Christian
The Foundation
    The Servants of the Christ
    The Saints in the City
    The Soldiers of the Church
    The Salutation of the Cross
The Friendship
    The Prisoner's Appreciation
    The Prayerful Appeal
    The Pleased Apostle
The Fellowship
    The Genesis of the Church
    The Gifts from the Christians
    The Guarantee from the Christ
The Fight
    The Grounds for His Confidence
    The Gains from Their Courage
    The Gloom of His Confinement
The Formula
    The Basis of Love
    The Bounty of Love
    The Boundaries of Love

The Facts
    The Search Required
    The Sincere Relationship
    The Savior's Return
The Fruits
    The Righteousness of the Believer
    The Roots of the Believer
    The Rejoicing of the Believer

The Formation

The Background of the City

Philippi was a city in eastern Macedonia, named after Philip II of Macedonia, the father of Alexander the Great. Philippi was about ten miles from the Aegean Sea and seventy miles northwest of Thessalonica. It became a Roman colony in 42 B.C. after Mark Anthony and Octavian (Augustus Caesar) combined forces to defeat the armies of Brutus and Cassius (the assassins of Julius Caesar) at Philippi. Since it was a Roman colony, the Philippians were entitled to the rights and privileges of those who lived in the cities of Italy. One decade later, Octavian defeated the forces of Anthony and Cleopatra in a naval battle in Actium. As a result of this battle, Octavian punished the supporters of Anthony by evicting them from Italy and making them resettle in Philippi.

    On Paul's second missionary journey in A.D. 49, he made his first visit as a Christian to Philippi (Acts 16). Luke described Philippi as "the chief city of that part of Macedonia." He visited the city again on his third missionary journey (Acts 20:1, 6). As a result of his visits, the city would never be the same.

The Birth of the Church

According to Acts 16:9, Paul had a vision of a man from Macedonia begging him to come and help them. After the vision, he set sail for Europe. At Philippi, Paul found the first Christian congregation on European soil. When Paul and his partners arrived in Philippi, God had arrived before them to prepare the souls of the inhabitants to hear and receive the gospel. However, Paul and his companions faced some unusual challenges before revival took place in the lives of some of the people.

It all started with the *purple seller*. Normally, Paul would go to the local synagogue when he arrived in a new area. But this did not happen in Philippi. Many people believe there were not enough male Jews in this area to have a local synagogue. A minimum of ten men was required to have one. In Acts 16, we read of Paul joining a group of women down at the seaport. There, Lydia and other women were gathered on the Sabbath to worship. Paul sat down and talked to them, and as a result of her hearing the gospel message, Lydia's heart was opened and she received Jesus Christ. After she and her entire household were baptized, she extended the gift of hospitality to Paul and his companions.

The New Testament lists many wonderful women of the faith. Lydia must be included on the list. This woman from Thyatira was not only the first convert in Philippi and Macedonia; she was the first convert in all of Europe. Nor was she satisfied to receive Christ only for herself. She passed the information about Christ on to her family and others in her household. As a result, they received Christ—a revival had begun. The Bible describes her as a seller of purple. Lydia sold purple-dyed goods from as far away as Thyatira. Can you imagine Lydia using her business as a place to evangelize souls? I can see her placing a gospel tract about the salvific power of Jesus Christ in the bags of all of her customers. If we were to focus on leading one person to Christ at a time rather than trying to save the world, the world would eventually be covered.

After leading Lydia and her family to Christ, Paul and his ministry teammate came in contact with a *possessed sister* (Acts 16:16–18). As Paul and Silas were on their way to prayer, a girl possessed with a spirit of divination followed them proclaiming, "These men are the servants of the Most High God, who show us the way of salvation" (Acts 16:17). This grieved Paul. "What was wrong with what she was saying?" you may ask. It wasn't what she was saying but who was saying it through her that was the problem. Satan wanted these men of God to be seen as some kind of hoax. So Paul rebuked the evil spirit and it came out of her at that same hour. As a result of coming in contact with these men of God, the girl no longer had the ability to read crystal balls and palms. She was free from that evil spirit.

The text does not specifically say that she was saved and baptized. However, it is inferred later by the men who had used her as a pawn in the old days. They accused Paul and Silas of teaching customs that were unlawful to Romans. After her deliverance, the girl had probably gone back to tell them why she wouldn't be working for them any longer. I strongly believe that as a result of this missionary journey, a girl under the control of Satan became a follower of Christ. The story of the gospel is stronger than the grip of Satan.

We move from the delivered girl to the *prison scene*. The deliverance of the girl angered some people. This led to Paul and Silas being thrown in jail after being beaten with many stripes (Acts 16:23). The magistrates gave the jail keeper specific instructions to guard these Jewish prisoners safely or run the risk of losing his life. I love what Paul and Silas did once they were thrown into the inner prison. The passage says that they began to pray and sing praises to God. That is the right way to deal with the pains and perils of ministry. We should all learn how to praise God at midnight when something or someone has interfered with our mission. While they were singing and praying, the Bible says the other prisoners heard them (Acts 16:25). I don't know who was in jail that night, or for what crimes, but I believe they were blessed when that jail was transformed into a place of worship.

God caused an earthquake so that the foundation of the prison was shaken. The earthquake caused all of the cell doors to open. It is possible that the prisoners who heard Paul and Silas praising God received Christ as well that night. One of the reasons for saying this is what happened once all of the cell doors opened. None of the prisoners tried to escape. They had the opportunity but chose not to run. Perhaps it was due to some changed hearts.

The jail keeper was afraid that the prisoners had escaped, and drew his sword to take his own life. Paul assured him that all of the prisoners were accounted for. The next thing we hear is the jail keeper asking, "What must I do to be saved?" (Acts 16:30). When it was all said and done, the jailer and his household were saved and baptized.

When God permits trouble to come, He can still cause ministry to take place. There are times when the work of ministry leads to persecution. When it does, we should remain focused and faithful. Our commitment in the storm can cause others to give their lives to Christ.

Acts 16 closes by telling the reader about the *productive season* (Acts 16:40). Before Paul and Silas departed, they met with the brethren in the city. In other words, the church was birthed in

Philippi. This missionary journey that started as a vision ended as a victory for Paul and his companions.

The Bonds of the Christian

Paul is not sitting behind some desk in an office or at home as he writes this letter. The book of Philippians is one of the four shorter epistles written by Paul while he was in prison. (The other three are Ephesians, Colossians, and Philemon.) King Agrippa was responsible for sending Paul to Rome to be tried by Augustus after Paul made his appeal (Acts 26:32). So as Paul wrote this epistle, he was a prisoner in Rome.

Although he was bound in prison, he wrote this letter filled with joy. The theme of this writing could be "Joy in Christ." In the book of Philippians, the word rejoice is found nine times; the word joy, five times; and the expression to rejoice with, two times. Why was there so much joy in the life of a prisoner? Most people in prison write letters filled with doom and gloom. What caused this prisoner to be different? Did he realize that he could possibly die as a result of his imprisonment? It really didn't matter because nothing could rob Paul of the joy he had in Jesus Christ.

The Foundation (1:1–2)

The Servants of the Christ (1)

It is not uncommon for a letter in the New Testament to open with the first name of the writer mentioned. In Paul's letters, his name is always mentioned. In some cases, he listed the name of his companions like Timothy and Silvanus. When the letter was unsealed and the name of Paul was heard by the church members in Philippi, they would know exactly who the writer was. When Lydia and her family heard that name, they would probably start to reflect on the time Paul, Silas, and Timothy spent in their home. The Roman jail keeper would remember the night he had thought about committing suicide but Paul, the man of God, kept him from it. He would think about the fact that on that night not only did he not take his life, he also received eternal life.

The members at Philippi would also remember Paul's faithful minister. Timothy, half Jew and half Greek, was a faithful companion of Paul. He was willing to do whatever he could to help the gospel message spread. When an errand needed to be run for Paul,

Timothy would eagerly take care of it. He knew that his father in the ministry was sent out by God to plant the seed of the gospel all over the region. Timothy probably was honored to have the privilege of working with Paul. He probably felt even more honored to have Paul include his name in some of his letters to the churches planted on those missionary journeys.

Paul described himself and Timothy as "the servants of Jesus Christ." The humility of Paul is awesome. He didn't address himself as the "founding pastor" or the "organizing apostle" of the church at Philippi. He wanted the congregation to know that he was a servant of the Lord. Paul considered himself to be a slave to Christ. It was all about Jesus from his perspective. He was honored to have been chosen to serve as one of the many ambassadors of Jesus Christ. He knew he did not have any bragging rights. The experience on the Damascus road had changed that for him (Acts 9). When he gave his life to Christ, dignity and humility set in.

The Saints in the City

After the letter reveals the person from whom it was sent, the name or names of the addressee(s) are revealed. This letter is addressed first "to all of the saints in Christ Jesus which are at Philippi." The word saints means separated or holy ones. Who is Paul addressing with this term? He is addressing every man, woman, boy, and girl in Philippi who had accepted Jesus as Lord and Savior. As a matter of fact, he is even talking to those believers who were not necessarily living saintly lives.

When they are called saints, he is speaking positionally for all and practically for some. All believers are saints from a *positional* perspective. By receiving Jesus Christ in their lives, they were immediately justified to the Father through the Son. They became the recipients of imputed righteousness. He is also speaking to most of them from a *practical* perspective as well. As we shall see in the letter as we continue, Paul was pleased with the report of how the members of the Philippian family of faith were living.

As a believer, you are a saint. We become saints at the moment of conversion. It doesn't matter how we have sinned in the past. When our heavenly Father looks in our direction, He no longer sees us—He sees the blood of His Son that covers us. This causes us to be considered righteous saints. He also equips us to live according to the title. When Jesus died for our sins, His death dealt with the power of sin over us. Sin no longer has the power to control us. We are under new management.

The Soldiers of the Church

Next, Paul addresses the leadership in the church. When Paul planted churches on his missionary journeys, he did not leave without making sure they were organized properly. He made sure the churches had people in leadership positions. He knew that his charge was to start the local congregations. After starting the congregations, he would need to leave and go elsewhere to do the same thing. Although he planned to return on other missionary journeys, the congregations needed to have people in positions of leadership to carry out the church work in that congregation, as well as the work of the church in that city. Lack of structure is dangerous in any institution. When the Holy Spirit descended at Pentecost, "he gave some, apostles; and some, prophets; and some, evangelists; and some pastors and teachers; for the perfecting of the saints, for the work of the ministry for the edifying of the body of Christ" (Eph. 4:11–12).

The church is the army of God on earth. All of the saints are soldiers. You have captains, colonels, privates, etc. For the church, it is not about *rank* but about *responsibility*. It's not about *dominance* but about *duty*. The officers of this army are revealed in verse 1. They are the bishops and deacons. The Greek word for bishop is *episkopos*, meaning "overseer." The word for deacons is *diakonos*, which means "to provide service." One of the reasons for listing them after the saints is that pastors and deacons are God-ordained offices of the church. Both offices represent positions of servanthood.

The Salutation of the Cross (2)

Listen to the words of Paul's salutation. He says, "Grace be unto you, and peace, from God our Father, and from the Lord Jesus Christ" (1:2). The words "grace . . . and peace" in the greeting reveal the power of the cross. When Jesus died on the cross, the veil of the Temple was destroyed. This meant there would no longer be the need to have the high priest enter the Holy of holies on behalf of the people. The people had now gained direct access to the Father through the Son. In the past, the high priest had to go in and sprinkle blood on the mercy seat for the sins of the Jews. The death of Jesus put an end to this practice. The shed blood of Jesus closed one door and opened another. It closed the door of the high priest's role and opened the door for all people, including the non-Jew or Gentile race.

This salutation from Paul reveals the fact that there is no difference between the Jew and the Greek because the same God was rich unto all who called upon His name (Rom. 10:12). "Grace" is the Gentile greeting, and "peace" is the Jewish greeting. Every bornagain Gentile knew that it was because of grace that he was saved. The Jews were very familiar with the title of Father. They knew Jehovah as the Father of Abraham, Isaac, and Jacob. *Peace* was a common greeting among the Jews. However, it was the grace from the Son that initiated the peace from the Father for all.

The Friendship (1:3–4)

The Prisoner's Appreciation (3)

As you read this letter to the Philippians, it is evident that Paul loved and appreciated the saints in the church in Philippi. Of all the letters of Paul, this one is filled with words of intimacy and affection. The evidence of this love is seen in verse 3 where Paul says, "I thank my God upon every remembrance of you." There is always an attitude of gratitude when you love someone. The thought of the saints in Philippi caused Paul to be thankful. When he thought about them, the spirit of thanksgiving started flowing in his heart.

Thankfulness is always a sign of love. When you think of someone you love, you will be thankful for having him or her in your life. When you can be thankful every time you think of a group of people, the love is genuine. Paul was not saying that this church was the perfect church. He knew better than that, as we shall see later on in this letter. Although they were not perfect, they were genuine and faithful.

The Prayerful Appeal (4)

The imprisonment of Paul hindered him from traveling to see the saints. If Paul had not been incarcerated, I'm sure that his missionary journeys would have continued. Now, he is in chains. Although he couldn't visit them, he could visit someone else on their behalf. He says, "Always in every prayer of mine for you all making request with joy" (1:4). Those in charge of his imprisonment could keep him from physically leaving the premises to visit his friends. They could even intercept the letters that he wrote to his friends. At some point, they may have even discontinued the visits from his friends. One thing they could not do was stop him from praying for his friends.

Paul persistently prayed for them. As a matter of fact, he spent time praying for all of the churches established on his missionary journeys. Although Paul was in prison, he knew about some of the needs of the churches. During his prayer time, he would petition God on their behalf. Prison may have *hampered his preaching*, but it could not *hinder his praying*. In fact, Paul's imprisonment probably sharpened his prayer life. There are times when a period of isolation will lead to a special time of consecration and revelation. Paul probably communed with God more in prison that he did before. Those long hours in prison were not wasted but were used to pray for his friends.

The Pleased Apostle (4b)
When he prayed for them and petitioned God on their behalf, it was done with joy in his heart. When the Philippians surfaced on his prayer list, a smile probably appeared on his face. He was so pleased with this body of believers. When he thought of them, joy like a river started flowing in his soul. This was not the case with all of the churches on his prayer list. There were probably some other emotions he felt when the Ephesians or Corinthians surfaced on his list. In the case of the Philippians, it was always a joyous remembrance.

It is not that he loved this group of believers more than other groups. Paul loved the family of God. However, this church had a special place in his heart. He could not forget about the souls saved there when he made that trip to Asia. He could not forget about the love shown by them while he traveled as well as while he was in prison. Paul was pleased with this family of faith and enjoyed petitioning God on their behalf.

The Fellowship (1:5–6)

The Genesis of the Church (5)
In verse 5 he says, "From the first day. . . ." Paul is speaking of the day when he traveled on his second missionary journey. Although the vision came for him to go to Macedonia, he didn't have any idea how the Macedonians would respond to the preaching and teaching of the gospel. As he was sailing to this region, I am sure he worked on several sermons to be delivered while there he probably wondered which one he would preach. I am sure he wondered how he would cause an audience to gather to hear him preach and teach

the good news. He may have wondered if the people in Europe would reject or accept the gospel message.

Now as Paul reminisced about those first days, he probably had a smile on his face. Everything that he had wondered about, God had already worked out.

When he arrived, God had caused a group of people to congregate at the sea. After Paul preached and taught, a businesswoman and her household were saved. It appears that the most popular topic and text for his sermons was: "Believe on the Lord Jesus Christ, and thou shalt be saved, and thy house" (Acts 16:31). He remembered how the new believers immediately got involved in ministry. After Lydia and her family were saved and baptized, they immediately extended hospitality to Paul and others. After the jailer and his family were saved, he immediately started attending the wounds of Paul and Silas. From the beginning, they were with him all the way.

The Gifts from the Christians (5)

There is an old cliché that says, "Out of sight, out of mind." It had been ten years since he baptized Lydia and the others in Philippi. Although he had traveled there again on his third missionary journey, he had been away from them for a long time when this letter was written. Yet, he says that the partnership had continued ". . . until now." Yes, this partnership (fellowship) had not stopped even though Paul was in prison. After Paul left the believers in Philippi, they continued to show their appreciation to him for the work of ministry. His imprisonment did not keep them from fellowshipping with him. Although all of them could not come, they gladly helped to send others with gifts for the servant of God.

Isn't it wonderful to see people who were set on fire for Jesus years ago still carrying the torch? There have been many that started with a lot of zeal and fervor, but somewhere along the way they slowed down. At first, they were the ones who wanted to be a part of every extended service of the church. They volunteered for various ministries. But as time passed, they were not as visible as they once were. Before long, they were MIA (Missing in Action). This was not the case of the Philippians who had given their lives to Christ. They started with Paul ten years before, and the partnership had not stopped.

The Guarantee from the Christ (6)

First, Paul deals with the *rebirth of the sinner*. He says, "Being confident of this very thing, that he which hath begun a good work in you . . ." (1:6). Paul is addressing the first day when the different members of this church became members of the family of God. When Lydia accepted Christ as the Lord and Savior of her life, a good work was started in her. When the jailer received Christ in his life, a good work was started in him. When Jesus enters the hearts of men, a change of heart occurs. It is a new beginning. The hands of the believer are placed on the gospel plow. The feet of the believer are placed on the straight and narrow path.

Paul not only deals with the rebirth of the sinner, he also deals with the *reformation by the Spirit*. Paul says that the same power that led to the rebirth "will perform it until the day of Jesus Christ" (1:6). The *redemption* and *rebirth* occurs first and is followed up with *reformation*. The same Spirit that convicted the believer to repent and be saved will continue to dwell in the life of the believer. Not only does the Holy Spirit desire to dwell in the life of the believer, He desires to fill the life of the believer. As He starts taking over the life, reformation is seen in that life. The believer starts shedding more of the old and putting on more of the new.

After dealing with the reformation by the Spirit, Paul deals with *the rapture of the saints*. Paul was confident that the work that had started would continue until the church is raptured. The work Jesus started would continue until they all could hear Him say, "Well done." The Christians in the Philippian church were growing, glowing, and going in the name of Jesus. This would continue until the Lord came for all saints.

The Fight (1:7–8)

The Grounds for His Confidence (7)

Paul had a lot of confidence in this body of believers. The grounds for his confidence are seen in the courageous support they offered him as a prisoner. Paul says, "Even as it is meet for me to think this of you all, because I have you in my heart; . . . as both in my bonds" (1:7a). In other words, Paul was saying, "The reason I have this confidence in you is because you are not only in my heart, you are with me in this fight." The support of the Christians in Philippi was not hidden. They didn't mind showing their support for this man of God openly. They supported the man, the message, and the ministry.

This support of Paul could have been costly. Paul was preaching a message about someone he said was the King of kings and the Lord of lords. During that time in history, a message of that nature was considered treasonous. That message painted a picture that there was someone greater than Caesar. Anyone preaching such a message could have been considered as an insurrectionist. Anyone supporting a person preaching this message would also be considered a dissident or rebel toward the government. Paul was saying that this did not matter to his friends in Philippi.

The Gains from Their Courage (7b)

He continues by saying, "and in the defense and confirmation of the gospel, ye all are partakers of my grace" (1:7b). The Greek word for "defense" is *apologia* from which we derive our English word "apologetics." The word for "confirmation" is *bebaiosis*. It symbolizes a guarantee. Paul was looking forward to his hearing with the top man in the government. He was looking forward to this hearing not to find out if he would be found innocent or guilty. The reason he was looking forward to this audience was to present his argument for the eternal life that one can receive from the gospel. He was looking forward to presenting the gospel of our Lord and Savior Jesus Christ to Caesar.

Paul wanted the Christians at Philippi to know that their support of him was actually as if they were with him in witnessing to Caesar. For Paul, life was all about the gospel. This was the same for those Philippians who loved the Lord. In a real sense, it was as if the Philippians were witnessing to all of the people to whom Paul witnessed. Their courageous support caused them to be partakers of the same grace Paul enjoyed. Every time you support a missionary in a foreign land, it is almost as if you are there yourself.

The Gloom of His Confinement (8)

If there was anything gloomy about this state of affairs for Paul, it was the fact that he longed to be with his friends. The word "bowels" seems like the wrong word to use in describing how you miss someone. We must remember that in the past many words had meanings different from those we use today. This word is a perfect example of that rule. The word "bowels" comes from the Greek word *splancha*. It was a metaphor used to describe a person's deepest inner affections. Paul missed their physical fellowship. He wanted to dine once again at the home of Lydia and her family. He wanted to fellowship again with the entire church family in Philippi.

The Formula (1:9)

The Basis of Love

The Bible teaches that God is love. Since He is love, he can equip His children to love. Paul says, "And this I pray, that your love may abound" (1:9a). Paul knew that they loved him. He could see the demonstration of their love for him in so many ways. He tells them to continue down the same path. He needed that same love to flourish in the congregation. Paul sounds like Jesus in this verse. Jesus said to His disciples, "As the Father hath loved me, so have I loved you; continue ye in my love" (John 15:9). In John 13:35, Jesus says, "By this shall all men know that ye are my disciples, if ye have love one to another." Also, Paul had to plant this spiritual nugget in their hearts and minds because of a problem brewing in the church. He will be more specific later in this letter.

The Bounty of Love

Paul says, "And this I pray, that your love may abound yet more" (1:9b). Not only did he want that love to abound in the house of faith, he also wanted it to abound outside of the house of faith. In Mark 12:30-31, Jesus said, "And thou shalt love the Lord thy God with all thy heart, and with all thy soul. . . . And the second is this: Thou shalt love thy neighbor as thyself. There is none other commandment greater than these." He wanted them to share that same love with the world. A believer who is bitter toward an unbeliever will find it difficult to lead that person to Christ. That is why it is so important to keep the door of communication open between the believer and unbeliever. You never know when the unbeliever will enter through that open door as an unbeliever and exit as a believer because of your witness.

The Boundaries of Love

Paul says, "And this I pray, that your love may abound yet more and more in knowledge and in all judgment" (1:9). This abounding love that flowed from the hearts of the Philippians was to be extended both in knowledge as well as in judgment. The word *epignosis* used here deals with knowledge that is obtained by further examination or experience.

Although their love was to be bountiful, there also needed to be some boundaries in expressing that love. Yes, it was true that they needed to love all people—the believer as well as the unbeliever. However, there was a need for them to know some things about the people they loved, thus allowing the growth of that love to develop based on good judgment (discernment) in using that knowledge. They could love all people. But knowledge of these people and their ways should lead the believer to make a decision or judgment concerning the amount of love offered—and the way it is offered. If the person lives in sin, limited love should exist. The opposite is true as well. The more knowledge you have of a person's righteous ways, the freer you are to love him or her even more.

The Facts (1:10)

The Search Required (10a)

Paul's desire for the Philippians was "that ye may approve things that are excellent" (1:10a). The word for "approve" is *dokimazo* in the Greek. It means "to examine." The word "excellent" means "things that are different." Paul encouraged the believers at Philippi to examine the things that they heard. Everything that sounds true may not be true. It may be close or approximate and still be off track. As we examine things that are different, using the lens of what we already know from God's Word, the more we learn. This search for truth should be the mission of every believer. One of the characteristics of becoming a disciple of Christ is a determination to learn more about God's will for our lives.

The Sincere Relationship (10b)

The *appropriation* and *approximation* of truth must lead to the *application* of truth. Paul wanted the Philippians to "be sincere and without offence till the day of Christ" (1:10). Here Paul dealt with a danger that is prevalent today in the lives of many believers. It is possible to be sincere about faith but still be wrong because of the lack of knowledge regarding truth. It is also possible to be knowledgeable about truth but be insincere about it. Paul reminded the church at Philippi of the importance of being sincere and knowledgeable about the truth.

As believers, we should seek to take possession of the truth. Christianity is not about having a lot of philosophies and creeds by which to live. Christianity involves the continuous search for the truth. Once truth is found, the believer should grab it and hold onto it.

The Savior's Return (10c)

After testing and examining those things that are different, the believer must apply the truth. The Philippians needed to test the things that were different and commit to doing those things that were right. Paul wanted them to "be sincere and without offence till the day of Christ" (1:10). The knowledgeable believer must live according to the truth until the Lord returns. How sad it would be if He were to come back and find us knowledgeable of the truth and not living accordingly. It is like the reminder in the letter written to the church at Smyrna in Revelation 2:10 that we should be faithful until death or until the departure of the church.

When He returns, we want to be living in such a way that would not cause Him to be ashamed. This is why we should live every day as if He were returning on that day. The truth is that He can return for the church at any time. No one knows the hour when the Son of man will appear. Therefore, it would be wise for the church to act as if He were coming back today.

The Fruits (1:11)

The Righteousness of the Believer (11a)

Paul said he wanted the Philippians to be "filled with the fruits of righteousness" (1:11a). If the believer is not filled with the fruits of righteousness, it is impossible to live a righteous life. Someone has suggested that whatever you are full *of* will come *out of* you. Yes, it is true that God sees the believer as being righteous because he is covered with the blood of Jesus Christ. However, when others look at a believer, they don't see the covering. What they need to see is a display of righteousness flowing from the believer's life. When Paul wrote to the Corinthians, he said, "If any man be in Christ, he is a new creature; old things are passed away; behold, all things are become new" (2 Cor. 5:17). The fruit of the Spirit should be seen in our lives.

There should be some love blossoming on our branches. This love should be shown to all people. There should be joy, peace, longsuffering, and all the other fruit of the Spirit growing on our branches. There should be a noticeable change in one's life after becoming a child of the King. One of the greatest tests for a believer is to come in contact with someone from his or her past—from the "before Christ" (B.C.) days. When that person from the past says, "You have really changed," that is a good sign. Or, when someone says, "You are really serious about the church business," that is a good sign. It is always good for people to detect a noticeable difference, especially those who don't believe.

The Roots of the Believer (11b)

The enemy will try to convince the believer that he cannot live a righteous life. He will remind him of the past life and how difficult it was to stay on the straight and narrow.

God knew the enemy would try to convince us that righteous living is impossible. Therefore, the Holy Spirit had Paul inform us that the success of righteous living is not contingent on our personal power not to sin. Paul tells us that the fruits of righteousness "are by Jesus Christ" (11b). In John 15:5, Jesus says, "I am the vine, ye are the branches. He that abideth in me, and I in him, the same bringeth forth much fruit; for without me ye can do nothing." When there has been an *inward metamorphosis*, there will be an *outward manifestation*.

Branches cannot produce anything on their own. A branch is powerless by itself. If you detach a branch from the tree, the branch dies. It can only survive if it is connected to the tree. In a spiritual sense, we have the same formula for righteousness. The power over sin flows from the vine to the branches. The fruits of righteousness can only be produced when you are rooted and grounded in Jesus Christ. He is the one who causes the believer to start living like a saint.

The Rejoicing of the Believer (11c)

The righteous living is to be done "unto the glory and praise of God" (1:11c). Paul wanted the Christians at Philippi to rejoice and give God the glory for their changed lives. The righteous behavior of a believer is not to be viewed as some undesirable chore. Instead, the believer rejoices in being given the ability to do in Christ what he could not do on his own. He renders praise to God for the victorious life. God is able to get the glory when He is able to see us living in a way that is pleasing to Him. He did not create us to live in sin. He desires to see us conformed to the image of His Son.

CHAPTER 2

Addressing Adversity and the Adversary

Philippians 1:12–19

The Divine Plan
    The Spreading of the Word
    The Shackles of the Witness
    The Strength for the Weak
The Different Preachers
    The Pretenders in the Pasture
    The Passion of the Preacher
    The Purpose of the Pretense
    The Performance of His Partners
The Dedicated Prisoner
    The Results of Their Preaching
    The Rejoicing of the Prisoner
    The Reliance on the Prayers
    The Reaction to the Persecution

The Divine Plan (1:12–14)

The Spreading of the Word (12)

Paul had to clarify an issue for those saints in Philippi. He did not want them to misinterpret the things that had transpired in his life. They did not need to sit around and cry over his imprisonment. Paul said, "But I would ye should understand, brethren, that the things which happened unto me have fallen out rather unto the furtherance of the gospel" (1:12). Paul wanted the Philippians to praise God for what had taken place in his life. His missionary trips may have stopped but his ministry had not been stifled. While in prison, he was still able to lead many souls to Christ. In a real sense, his imprisonment was probably better than what he encountered on the missionary journeys. In prison, he didn't have to deal with strong winds, stormy seas, or shipwrecks.

From the beginning of the church's history, Satan has tried to keep the good news from spreading. But every time Satan has tried to do something to hinder the spreading of the gospel, it has backfired. He tried accusation when the church began on the day of Pentecost. The people in Jerusalem that day accused the 120 people who were filled with the Holy Spirit of being drunk from drinking new wine. Satan's trick was squashed and over 3,000 souls were added to the church (Acts 2:41).

Next, he tried to divide the church by creating a problem between the Greek and Hebrew Christians in Acts 6. As a result, the seven deacons were selected. The next thing you read about is the powerful witness of two of these deacons—Stephen and Philip.

Even in Paul's ministry, Satan tried to prevent the gospel from spreading. When Paul and Barnabas split up over the matter regarding John Mark, Satan thought he had blocked the mission. Instead of blocking the mission, he ended up helping the mission. Paul and Silas went one way to spread the gospel and Barnabas and John Mark went another way to spread the gospel (Acts 15:36–40).

When you are walking in the will of God, you don't have to worry about the things that befall you. If being in the will of God led you into your situation, God can use you there. It may not be the work environment that you prefer, but God has a plan to use you to change that environment. You may feel imprisoned in the neighborhood where you live, but God can use you to help turn that neighborhood upside down.

There is a young man in our congregation who is very impressive. He is one of the most brilliant African-Americans I know. He received his doctorate from one of the top Ivy League schools in our country. He serves as the principal of a private elementary school in south Dallas. The school is located in an area that has been considered one of the top areas for criminal activity. With his skills and educational background, Dr. Terry Flowers could certainly find a much better job and make much more money. Yet, he has decided to stay at the school.

At first, I couldn't understand it. But after visiting the neighborhood some months ago, I discovered why he decided to stay. It wasn't just a job to Dr. Flowers; it was a ministry. In areas where crack houses once existed, there are now playgrounds. Houses that were once considered unlivable and in need of condemnation have been restored, and the neighborhood looks like a million dollars. The children attending the school have some of the best test scores in the city.

If you are where God has placed you, then you are in the right place. Let your light shine in that place no matter how unpleasant the environment. God has a plan and He desires to use you in that plan. So, instead of trying to escape, let God use you to impact someone's life.

The Shackles of the Witness (13)

Paul wrote, "So that my bonds in Christ are manifest in all of the palace, and in all other places" (1:13). As a result of Paul's imprisonment, Rome was blessed. Paul took every advantage to spread the good news of our Lord and Savior Jesus Christ. When the soldiers were placed in the cell to guard him, Paul probably started preaching and teaching. Every four hours or so, another guard would come in and relieve the other. I am sure there were times when one guard said to another guard, "Listen, I'll go ahead and work your shift so that I can finish listening to this lesson that Paul is teaching me about faith." Then when the soldier got off duty, he would go home and teach his family everything he had heard. Some of those same soldiers also had the duty of working in the palace. There they would dispense the good news Paul had shared with them to those in royal positions.

When the Christians in Rome assembled to worship, they noticed that the membership continued to grow. On testimony night, people would probably stand and share how the message of the gospel shared by Paul with their husbands, brothers, uncles, etc. had caused them to see the light and give their lives to Jesus Christ.

The Strength for the Weak (14)

As a result of Paul's bondage, he could see the affect it was having on other believers. Paul wrote that "many of the brethren in the Lord, waxing confident by my bonds, are much more bold to speak the word without fear" (1:14). Paul's evangelistic enthusiasm became a tool of inspiration for other believers in Rome. The Christians in Rome were impressed with Paul's holy boldness. Here was a man in chains for his testimony. Instead of keeping his mouth closed about the saving power of Christ, he took advantage of every opportunity to tell someone about Jesus. His preaching and teaching of the gospel to the guards and others could have been used against him at his trial. This didn't matter to Paul. He was more concerned about people receiving Christ than he was about the outcome of his trial.

This boldness of Paul started spreading like wildfire. The man who had written a letter to the Romans from Corinth years ago was faithful to his calling. He was not ashamed of the gospel. If Paul could preach while in prison, they decided they could be bold like their leader. Paul's example was copied by others. His commitment became their commitment. They did not fear what would happen to them. They decided that if Paul could do it, so could they. One sign of a good leader is the ability to cause followers to become leaders. Because of Paul's boldness, these followers started leading people to Christ without fear or shame.

The Different Preachers (1:15–17)

The Pretenders in the Pasture (15a)

Not everyone was serious about ministry. Paul says, "Some indeed preach Christ even of envy and strife" (1:15a). There were some who were envious of Paul. They were jealous of Paul's success in the ministry. Paul was probably leading more people to Christ from prison than they were from their pulpits. People were coming back to the church with a new determination for Christ. Although Paul's ministry was helping the body of Christ, some had become envious of Paul's effectiveness.

There was not only envy, there was also strife. Envy always leads to strife. When there is jealousy and bitterness, you can expect discord and division to surface. Strife is one of the by-products of envy. The word "strife" means "factious rivalry." Since there were preachers envious and jealous of Paul, an unhealthy spirit of competition surfaced. Instead of preaching the gospel, these preachers probably spent all of their time preaching against Paul. They were more concerned about turning people against Paul than they were in turning people on to the truth. Every time someone boasted about the effective ministry of Paul, these anti-Paul preachers would probably start bashing Paul's ministry.

In a small town in Arkansas, a young evangelist came through and had what they call a "camp meeting." He had his tent set up in the worst part of the city. As he preached from under that tent, people who had planned to go out to party in social clubs heard him preaching and were compelled to go over and listen to him instead of going out to the clubs. Night after night, people flocked to the camp meeting. After three weeks of this camp meeting, some local pastors met to discuss what was going on. Some of the pastors called this man an irate evangelist, trying to take over the town. Some of the other pastors said that he was there trying to get money. After a brief discussion, they decided to tell the members of their churches to inform their friends and relatives in the town to stay away from him.

Just before that meeting ended, a young pastor walked in and was briefed on the decision of the other pastors. The young pastor said that he could not announce this from his pulpit on Sunday. The moderator of the group wanted to know the reason why he couldn't do it. The young pastor replied, "For the last three Sundays, we have had more people join our church as candidates for baptism. These are the people who have given their lives to Jesus Christ as a result of this irate evangelist's preaching."

After he said this, some of the other pastors started thinking about the unusual increase in their memberships over the last few Sundays. They came to the realization that this evangelist was not only leading people to Christ, he was directing these new converts to the local congregations as well. Instead of going through with their plans, the pastors spent the last week attending the camp meeting and doing all they could to help lead others to Christ. There is never room for envy and strife.

The Passion of the Preacher (15b)

There were others who were sincere. Paul says, ". . . and some also of good will" (1:15b). This group had a passion for the lost. These preachers had a heart desire to win the world for Christ. They were the ones excited about the life-changing preaching and teaching of Paul. As a matter of fact, they may have been the ones who planted the seed of faith and believed Paul simply came along and watered and fertilized the seed. Those who preach from good will see other preachers as partners in the overall plan of God.

When you have a heart for the ministry, it doesn't matter if someone else is leading more souls to Christ than you. You are just excited that souls are being saved. When there is preaching from good will, the salvation of souls is the only concern. The more preachers, the better. We are supposed to be involved in a *compelling ministry* rather than a *competitive market*.

It is disturbing to see jealousy and strife in the pulpit. When preachers of good will see the ministry of someone else striving and thriving, they simply praise God for it. There is never room for envy and strife. If the preacher's effectiveness is based on the Word of God, he should praise God for the number of souls being saved. Don't allow the *method* and *ministry* of another disturb you as long as the *message* is the same.

The Purpose of the Pretense (16)

Paul revealed the purpose connected to those who were pretenders. He said, "The one preach Christ of contention, not sincerely, supposing to add affliction to my bonds" (1:16). For these competitive-minded preachers, it was all about creating havoc for Paul. For them, it was more about irritating Paul than saving souls. If souls were saved in the process, that was OK. If Paul was stressed out as a result of their speaking, that was better. Their ultimate goal was to make Paul as miserable as possible. These preachers were so mean-spirited that they hoped it would increase his affliction. They wanted Paul to experience additional pain and even used his confinement to help their evil cause. They probably said things like, "If Paul is all that he preached about, he wouldn't be a jailbird." Perhaps they thought their negative comments about Paul and his ministry would cause him to become a miserable preacher in prison.

It is evident that they did not care much about Paul or much about Paul's God. Paul had majored in a course called "Affliction 101." After learning about the sufficiency of God's grace, Paul said, ". . . Most gladly, therefore, will I rather glory in my infirmities, that the power of Christ may rest upon me. Therefore, I take pleasures in infirmities, in reproaches, in necessities, in persecutions, in distresses for Christ's sake; for when I am weak, then am I strong" (2 Cor. 12:9–10). In other words, instead of making things worse for Paul, they were simply causing him to rejoice and become stronger in Christ.

You may be wondering what you should do when you know that others are trying to add affliction to your already difficult situation that is already difficult. The first response to that question is that you should never do what they are doing. You should seek to *live peaceably*. In 1 Thessalonians, Paul said, "See that none render evil for evil unto any man, but ever follow that which is good, both among yourselves, and to all men" (1 Thess. 5:15). Years before Paul had written, "Recompense to no man evil for evil. Provide things honest in the sight of all men. If it be possible, as much as lieth in you, live peaceably with all men" (Rom. 12:17–18).

Not only should you *live peaceably*, you should *love perfectly*. The Bible teaches that we should love our enemies and those who persecute us. Jesus said, "But I say unto you, Love your enemies, bless them that curse you, do good to them that hate you" (Matt. 5:44).

Lastly, you should *lobby prayerfully*. The last part of Matthew 5:44 says, ". . . and pray for them who despitefully use you, and persecute you." When love flows from the heart, your prayer list will include the enemy. When you pray for them, you should lobby on their behalf. Pray for change rather than condemnation.

The Performance of His Partners (17)

Paul then discussed the reason some preached out of good will. They were those who had a passion like him. He said, ". . . of love, knowing that I am set for the defense of the gospel" (1:17). Paul talked about his foes in verse 16. But now he wanted to share a word about his partners in the ministry. When a person is genuine, it requires others who are genuine to understand and render support. Paul knew not to expect unholy people to understand holy things. He knew not to expect the natural and carnal man to understand the spiritual man.

Paul wanted to make it clear that there were some holy and spiritual men standing on his side. They realized that Paul was not in prison because he deserved it. They recognized his imprisonment as a part of God's divine plan to get the gospel message out. They also realized that the effects of his imprisonment were far-reaching. They knew that because Paul was in prison, he would have the opportunity to witness to people they could never reach. The end result of more people being saved pleased them.

There are times when it appears as if we are in this thing called ministry alone. However, there are others around who God will allow to surface in time. Every time a pretender appeared during Paul's ministry, God probably allowed several authentic ministers to surface. He will always give us others who are "on the same page" as we are.

The Dedicated Prisoner (1:18–19)

The Results of Their Preaching (18a)

Although their *motives* were wrong, the *message* was right. Whenever a person tells the good news of the gospel, it is a good thing.

The story is told about a homeless brother who wanted to enter the mission one evening for a meal. Some of the other homeless people told him there was no way for him to get in if he hadn't checked in earlier. There were several homeless people in this area and the mission could not accommodate them all. This guy was high on drugs and didn't really want to stay in the mission. All he wanted was to get in long enough for a meal. He went to the door of the mission and begged the man to let him in to attend the worship service that night. He said, "I need to hear the Word of God tonight." Although the mission was full, after all the pleading and begging, the man at the door decided to let him in.

The man couldn't wait until the preacher finished his sermon. All he wanted to do was sit down and eat. Every now and then, the preacher would say something that sounded good and the man would clap and say, "That's right, Preacher." When the preacher sat down, the man said, "Amen." He didn't say it because he enjoyed the sermon; he was simply ready to eat and then get out of there and hang with the rest of his homeless brothers. After he finished his meal, he headed toward the door. The man at the door told him that he had to stay in for the night. After using a few choice words, he was allowed to exit.

After a few minutes, he caught up with another homeless brother to tell him about what he had just done. There were ten or so homeless men gathered around a fire burning in a can. "I told you I could get in," he boasted. He said that all he did was pretend to be accepting every word the preacher was saying. He said, "The preacher talked about God's Son dying on the cross to save men from their sins." Continuing, he said, "The preacher said if you want to be forgiven of your sins and saved from your sins, get up from where you are and come bow for the repentant prayer." He went on to tell them that a lot of people got up, and then he knew it was time to eat. As he laughingly told them what had happened, two men around that fire fell to their knees and repented of their sins and asked Jesus to save their souls. This man ended up leading some brothers to Christ without responding to the message himself.

Paul said, "What then? notwithstanding, every way, whether in pretence, or in truth, Christ is preached" (1:18a). Paul knew that their pretense would still lead to someone receiving Christ. The message of Christ was still going forward.

The Rejoicing of the Prisoner (18b)

Paul says, ". . . I therein do rejoice, yea, and will rejoice" (1:18b). Paul was so excited that the gospel was being preached. He allowed the preaching of the gospel to keep his mind off of those who were against him. When you can focus on the *preaching of the message* rather than *preachers of the message*, you can rejoice. Although some of the preachers were envious and jealous of him, Paul knew that the gospel was being preached to the Romans. This caused the prisoner to rejoice in his chains. In a nutshell, Paul was saying, "I have rejoiced, and I will continue to rejoice."

Paul's philosophy of ministry would be a good one for every child of God to adopt. When there are negative things taking place, we can try to focus on the positive. We should never allow the devil to think that he is winning. Yes, he will try to cause us to become disgusted, depressed, and disappointed. We should never allow him to interfere with our periods of praise. As a matter of fact, when he increases his assaults against us, we should increase our praise to the Lord.

The Reliance on the Prayers (19a)

Paul realized why he could stand so boldly. He had some friends lifting him up in prayer. He said, ". . . Through your prayer, and the supply of the Spirit of Jesus Christ" (1:19a). When you have prayer partners and the Spirit's powerful presence, you can make it through anything. Paul did not hear the prayers of the saints in Philippi, but he knew they were praying. He knew that someone had to be spending time praying for him because of the supernatural ability that surfaced in his life. Paul was writing this to make sure that they continued to pray for him.

When we pray for one another, we will have the powerful presence of the Spirit working overtime in our lives. We will be able to do things that are naturally impossible. We will be able to take in stride things from others that we couldn't normally deal with on our own. I have witnessed this time and time again in my ministry. I have been able to smile while being criticized and condemned by others. I have been able to preach and teach while some mean-spirited people were staring me down. This is because of some people taking the time to pray for me and for the ministry for which I am commissioned. I tell the members of the church where I serve to keep praying for me and to continue to call my entire name out when they do it.

The Reaction to the Persecution (19b)

Paul said, "I know that this shall turn to my salvation . . ." (1:19b). When Paul said, "I know," he used the Greek word, *oida*. The word means "absolute knowledge." Because of what he knew, Paul was not worried about the character assassinations. Can you imagine one of Paul's partners in the ministry visiting him in the prison one day? He might have said, "Brother Paul, I am fed up with those preachers trying to destroy your character. It is so unfair."

Paul may have looked this brother in the eye and said, "Do you remember what I wrote to you years ago?" He reminded him of what he had written in his letter to them: "And we know that all things work together for good to them that love God, to them who are the called according to his purpose. . . . What shall we then say to these things? If God be for us, who can be against us?" (Rom. 8:28, 31).

Paul wasn't worried about the things being said about him. Since God was for him, it didn't matter who was against him. He knew that he would win in the end. He knew this because it was predestined by God to work together for the good. When you know that you are in the will of God, you know that vindication will come. Vindication does not necessarily mean that you will not witness Nero's chopping block. It means that you will ultimately fulfill the divine purpose for your life.

When we are persecuted for righteousness' sake, we should take the same stand that Paul took in the text. We should learn to go with what we know. I know that my Redeemer is alive. I know that God is able. I know that things will work out for the good. I know that nothing can separate me from His love. I know He will keep me in perfect peace as long as my mind is stayed on Him.

CHAPTER 3

Living in the Lord

Philippians 1:20–30

The Difficult Crossroads
    The Duty of the Believer
    The Destiny of the Believer
    The Decision for the Believer
    The Desire of the Believer
The Divine Choice
    The Side of Sacred Duty
    The Strengthening of Special Disciples
    The Scene of Spiritual Development
The Discipleship Course
    The Conduct of the Church
    The Conformity of the Christian
    The Chronicling of Their Commitment
The Dangerous Calling
    Courage to Encounter Storms
    Courage to Endure Suffering
    Courage to Expect Struggling

The Difficult Crossroads (1:20–23)

The Duty of the Believer (20–21a)

Paul says, "According to my earnest expectation and my hope, that in nothing I shall be ashamed, but that with all boldness, as always, so now also Christ shall be magnified in my body, whether it be by life, or by death" (1:20). There are three things revealed in this verse that will affect the duty of the Christian. First of all, the text deals with *the character of a Christian*. Paul said that he was not going to be ashamed of anything. He was willing to live a holy and righteous life before anyone and everyone. It didn't matter if it were before other prisoners, guards, or dignitaries. He refused to be ashamed of his faith. We should never be ashamed to own up to our relationship with Christ. The Bible tells us in Luke 9:26 that if we are ashamed to own Him before men, He will be ashamed to own us before His Father and the angels.

Next, the text deals with *the courage of a Christian*. Not only was Paul determined not to be ashamed, neither was he going to allow fear to keep him from letting his light shine. It is true that Paul's courageous testimony would eventually lead to his death, but it really didn't matter. Paul refused to allow the spirit of fear to control his life. Many people fear what others will say and do if they know about their relationship with Christ. Paul did not allow chains, guards, or prison to keep him from living the life God had desired for him. It is true that this courageous testimony would possibly be used against him in future courts. But from Paul's perspective, the righteous Judge—and not any man—was the one to please. This holy boldness can only exist when the Spirit of God is in complete control of one's life.

Lastly, the text deals with *the Christ-likeness of a Christian*. All Paul wanted to do was to magnify Christ in his body. He wanted people to look in his direction to see what it really meant to be a Christian. When we claim to be Christians, we are saying that we are trying to be like Christ. The term does not simply identify who we are; it should also identify what we are about. For Paul, life was all about Jesus. His goal in life was to make sure that people saw Jesus through his life. In Philippians 1:21a, he says, "For to me to live is Christ. . . ." Paul wanted to be Christ-centered in every way and on every day in his life. He vowed to do whatever was necessary to cause people to see his wonderful Lord and Savior. He wanted his life to reflect the life of Christ even if this meant dying for the cause, just as his Savior had.

The Destiny of the Believer (21b)

Paul says, "For to me to live is Christ, and to die is gain" (1:21). Why does Paul speak of death in a positive light rather than a negative one? The answer is simple. If you are for Christ, you will eventually die in Christ if the Lord delays His coming. Dying in Christ is a blessing and not a burden. Dying in Christ is all about gains and not losses. The reason death is a decided gain for the believer is because the Bible says, "Precious in the sight of the LORD is the death of His saints" (Psa. 116:15). In a real sense, the believer does not die; he simply sleeps or rests from his labor.

There are three types of death in Scripture. There is the *physical death* of the body. There is the *spiritual death* which is man's separation from God because of his sinful state. Lastly, there is the *second death*, the eternal separation from God due to the sentencing by the righteous Judge.

The Decision for the Believer (22)
Paul says, "But if I live in the flesh, this is the fruit of my labour: yet what I shall choose I wot not" (1:22). The choice between life and death was not Paul's call. It was in God's hand. If God wanted him to remain in the flesh, he would continue to labor on behalf of Christ. The word "wot" is *gnoriza*, which means "to declare" or "to make known." Paul was making it perfectly clear that he was willing to do whatever the Lord wanted him to do. If God wanted him to live in the flesh, it meant that there was more work for him to do in life. If God permitted that he should die, it simply meant that his assignment in this life had been completed. Not only could Paul not make that call, neither could Caesar or any other man. God had the final say-so on the matter. The decision between life and death rests solely in the hands of the Almighty.

When we recognize the fact that life and death is God's decision, we will not allow the enemy to cause us to worry when we walk through the valley of the shadow of death. If it is time to go, God will decide. If it is not time to go, there is still work to be done.

The Desire of the Believer (23)
Paul says, "For I am in a strait betwixt two, having a desire to depart, and to be with Christ; which is far better" (1:23). First, we have *the lingering suspense*. Paul did not know exactly what would happen in the days ahead. He was really in suspense regarding the actions that would ultimately be taken by God. Was he going to stay to continue the work of ministry? Or, was he going to die

physically and depart for heaven? He didn't know the answer. He didn't know if there was another missionary journey in his future or not. He could not predict the future. By the way, since Paul could not predict the future, don't believe any of these others who claim to have that ability.

Next, he reveals *the lustful spirit*. The word "desire" in Greek is *epithumia*. It means "to lust after." Although he had a lingering suspense regarding his future, his desire was to go ahead and witness martyrdom. He was not trying to escape his earthly mission. He simply knew what awaited him in glory. Paul knew that this world was not his home. Earth was merely a temporary dwelling place for him.

Lastly, Paul deals with being on *the Lord's side*. The main reason he lusted after heaven was because he wanted to be present with the Lord. He longed to be with his Savior. His main concern was not on the mansions or pearly gates. He wanted to be with the Lord. When he wrote to the church at Corinth, he said, "Therefore, we are always confident, knowing that, while we are at home in the body, we are absent from the Lord. . . . We are confident, I say, and willing rather to be absent from the body, and to be present with the Lord" (2 Cor. 5:6, 8). There is nothing on this earth greater than being with the Lord. Many of us would love to have the loved ones who have gone before to be with us. They would not trade places with us for anything in the world.

The Divine Choice (1:24–26)

The Side of Sacred Duty (24)

Although Paul had a desire to go to heaven, he knew the benefits of staying on earth. He says, "Nevertheless to abide in the flesh is more needful for you" (1:24). His desire was to be with the Lord, but he knew there was a special and sacred duty for him to perform on earth. Paul still had some work to do on earth. The time of his departure had not arrived. There were more letters to write. There were more souls to point to the Lord.

We should keep our minds focused on what God has called us to do. When it is time for our fight to end, God will take care of it. We should be so committed to the call of ministry that when the end comes, we will be found doing what He commissioned us to do.

The Strengthening of Special Disciples (25)

Paul knew that the Lord wanted him to remain on earth so that the Philippians and others could continue to develop in the faith. Paul says, "And having this confidence, I know that I shall abide and continue with you all for your furtherance and joy of faith" (1:25). Paul deals with his *confidence*. Paul had confidence in the fact that he was still needed. Paul believed that the time of his departure had not yet arrived. He had confidence in his *continuance*. Although Nero was a madman, Paul knew that life for him would continue. God had placed this deep-rooted assurance in the heart of Paul. It was best for Paul's life to continue for another season.

Next, he deals with his *commission*. He did not have this confidence in his continuance just because he didn't want to die. His confidence of continuing was based on what he had been commissioned to do. He was needed so they could continue. When Paul speaks of their furtherance, he is talking about their spiritual journey. The church was on the move for Christ and his continuation would help the church to continue moving in the right direction.

The Scene of Spiritual Development (26)

Paul says, "That your rejoicing may be more abundant in Jesus Christ for me by my coming to you again" (1:26). Paul hoped that the news of his continuance would lead to their *victory*. He had hoped his continuance would cause their rejoicing in Christ to be more abundant. His continuance would also lead to his *visit*. Paul wanted his friends to know that he missed them and that he looked forward to seeing them again. He wanted to do more than send a letter; he wanted to come himself.

In essence, this verse reveals the *vision* of Paul. He could see himself arriving at the port of Philippi and traveling around nine miles to the town. He could see his friend Lydia selling her goods and running over to greet him. He could see all of the smiles on the faces of his friends. He could see a group of saints who had matured in the faith since his last visit. The sight of their spiritual development would make it all worthwhile.

The Discipleship Course (1:27)

The Conduct of the Church (27a)

Paul says, "Only let your conversation be as it becometh the gospel of Christ . . . (1:27). The word "conversation" has changed through the years. When Paul used the word, he was talking about their conduct and not just their verbal discussion. The word means "citizenship" or "manner of living." It deals with the walk that complements the talk. The true Christian is determined in what he does and not just in what he says. A person who says that he is a Christian should live a certain way. Have you ever heard someone say, "And you call yourself a Christian"? This is usually a statement that follows some unholy act done by a person who claims to be a Christian.

It is true that a Christian is not sinless, but if he is genuine he should be sinning less and less. It should be easy for the world to distinguish Christians from others in the world. The conduct of the Christian should give him away every time. America is known as the great melting pot of this world. There are so many people of different races, creeds and nationalities living here. Many foreigners living here bring with them the rituals and practices of the homeland and implement them here. Although they live in this country, you can tell they are from another country. This should be the same for the Christian. There should be a noticeable difference, revealing to the world that we are citizens of another world.

The Conformity of the Christian (27b)

The conduct of a Christian should conform to the "gospel of Christ" (1:27b). In the book of Acts, believers were identified as followers of the way. At Antioch, they were first called Christians. Both descriptions were used to identify these groups as followers of Jesus Christ. Paul said that the conduct of the believer should be "as it becometh the gospel of Christ . . ." (1:27b)—a reference to the Word of God. The Word of God is the standard by which to measure our conduct.

When we grow as believers, we should see our lives being conformed more and more into the image of His Son. Years before, when Paul wrote to the Romans, he said, "For whom he did foreknow, he also did predestinate to be conformed to the image of his Son . . ." (Rom. 8:29). When we apply the truth of the gospel to our lives, the picture of Christ is being developed in our lives.

When Peter decided to follow Jesus as the soldiers dragged Him from judgment hall to judgment hall, he ended up being accused of a being a follower of Christ. Two of his accusers said that he was with Jesus. Out of all of those sitting around the fire, they were able to pick Peter out as being a follower of Christ. Another accuser said that he sounded like one of them. (See Matthew 26:69–75.) It is good when the world can identify you as a follower of Jesus Christ.

The Chronicling of Their Commitment (27c)

Paul says, ". . . that whether I come and see you, or else be absent, I may hear of your affairs . . ." (1:27c). Paul wanted to make sure that this charge to them was not based on whether he was able to visit or not. He wanted to receive the news that their conduct was pleasing to the Lord at all times. It is good when a leader receives news that a group he had led to the Lord is demonstrating what it really means to be a disciple of Jesus Christ. When Paul reveals the information in this verse, he gives us the first strong indication of the problem that existed in the church of Philippi because of the disagreement between two women that he discusses later in chapter 4.

There are three things he wanted to hear about this church. Paul says, ". . . that ye stand fast in one spirit, with one mind striving together for the faith of the gospel" (1:27c). He wanted to hear about the *unity in their stance*. Paul wanted them to "stand fast." This is a common phrase used by Paul in his writings. In 1 Corinthians 16:13, he said, "Watch, stand fast in the faith, quit you like men, be strong." In Galatians 5:1, he says, "Stand fast, therefore, in the liberty wherewith Christ has made us free, and be not entangled again with the yoke of bondage." Later on, when he really deals with the problem in the Philippian church, he says, ". . . So stand fast in the Lord, my dearly beloved" (4:1). In 1 Thessalonians 3:8, he says, "For now we live, if we stand fast in the Lord." In 2 Thessalonians 2:15, he says, "Therefore, brethren, stand fast, and hold the traditions which ye have been taught, whether by word or our epistle."

He also wanted to hear about their *unity in the Spirit*. It is impossible to stand fast in the faith without the Holy Spirit being there to hold you up. When we become unified in the Spirit, everything in life begins to focus on Christ. The Holy Spirit allows us to get along when we normally would have conflict with one another.

Normally when we read Acts 3, we think that the only miracle in the chapter is connected to the lame man who was healed. However, in Acts 3, the first miracle is seen in the first verse where we read of Peter and John going together to the prayer meeting. In a real sense, this was a miracle because of the personalities involved. By nature, they were opposites because their temperaments were so different. Normally, people as different as these two fellows would not fellowship with each other. However, there was something that happened in Acts 2 that caused them to be able to get along. In Acts 2, they were both filled with the Holy Spirit. When the Spirit of God controls your life, you can get along with people of different temperaments.

Lastly, he wanted to hear about the *unity in their striving*. When Paul told them to "strive together," he used a word from which we get our word "athlete." They needed to have one mind in order to win the race before them. They could not allow the distractions and detours of Satan to cause them to get off track. They needed to strive together in order to accomplish the task assigned by the Lord through His Word. When there is dissonance, discord, and divisions, Satan is preventing the believer from focusing on the race. It is difficult for Satan to win when the church is united. Satan desires to switch the letters "i" and "t" in the word "united." The word "united" becomes the word "untied." An "untied church" will not be focused on the Word of God.

That is the news Paul wanted to hear about this family of faith in Philippi. The word he had received was different. There was friction in the house and they needed to get back on track and become unified. What are people saying about the church you are in? What is the word out there on you? Is the news spreading that there is a strong group of believers standing up for their beliefs? Someone is saying something about you whether you hear it or not. It would be good if the word out there is that yours is a group that is serious about the faith. It would be wonderful to hear that the church you are involved in is living according to the Word of God.

The Dangerous Calling (1:28–30)

Courage to Encounter Storms (28)

Paul says, "And in nothing terrified by your adversaries: which is to them an evident token of perdition, but to you of salvation, and that of God" (1:28). First, Paul deals with *the bravery test*. After challenging the saints to stand fast and strive together in the Spirit, he warns them of the impending danger from the enemies of the cross. Paul was telling them not to be afraid of anything that the enemy tried to do to them as they walked on the path of faith. Paul wanted them to know that there were storms in store for them as they attempted to live according to the Word of God. Their courage would be tested along the way.

For most of us, this bravery test is difficult to understand. Most of us have not been persecuted for righteousness' sake. We may have had our feelings hurt by being called a religious fanatic or a holy roller, but Paul is dealing with something much deeper. When you study church history, you learn about believers down through the ages who had their courage tested. Many of them were martyred for their belief. Although they faced danger, including death, they remained determined to keep their heads held high. They did not allow the threat of the adversary to prevent them from letting their lights shine. Paul didn't know it at the time, but he too would be added to that long martyrdom list.

Next, he deals with *the bully's torment*. As a result of the persecution of believers, the persecutor was in trouble. The word "perdition" means "destruction" or "damnation." The Bible reveals that the day of reckoning will come. In Romans 12:19, Paul said, "Vengeance is mine; I will repay, saith the Lord." In 2 Thessalonians 1:6, 8, Paul says, "Seeing it is a righteous thing with God to recompense tribulation to them that trouble you.... In flaming fire taking vengeance on them that know not God, and that obey not the gospel of our Lord Jesus Christ." The day will come when all enemies of the cross will be divinely dealt with.

This does not mean that every adversary of the cross is hellbound. As a matter of fact, the writer of this letter was once an enemy of the cross. Paul was saved while on his way to persecute the church. He was there when Stephen was being stoned to death. As he held the coats of the persecutors, he was there to hear every word spoken by Stephen. Stephen's behavior proved that he passed the bravery test. God probably allowed the scene of Stephen's bravery to reverberate in the mind of Paul. Paul's acceptance of Jesus Christ as Lord and Savior delivered him from the impending damnation that awaits the enemies of the cross.

The last thing Paul addresses in this verse is *the believers' testimony*. The bravery of the believers during the times of persecution became a testimony for others to see. When you can remain faithful during the time of persecution, it is one of the truest signals of being real. When you can die like Stephen and say, "Lord, please don't charge this to their account," it is a signal of a believer's authenticity. If you want to see how spiritual people really are, check them out when trouble comes. It is not difficult to hold your head up high when the sun is shining in your life. What happens when the clouds are hovering over? What happens when persecution comes?

The bravery of believers became a witness to those who are lovers of the cross. When you see other believers being faithful in the midst of persecution, it reveals that God will be there for you when your stormy days come. This is why I admire people who can praise God after witnessing some disastrous moment in life. I praise God along with them because I know if God can keep them strong in the midst of trouble, He can do the same for me.

Courage to Endure Suffering (29)

Paul says, "For unto you it is given in the behalf of Christ, not only to believe on him, but also to suffer for his sake" (1:29). When you read this verse, Paul makes it sound as if it is a privilege to suffer. He makes it sound like it is a blessing to be selected to suffer for Christ's sake. In a real sense, this is exactly what Paul is implying. The hymn writer said, "Must Jesus bear the cross alone, and all the world go free? No, there's a cross for everyone, and there's a cross for me." When the apostles were beaten with many stripes in the book of Acts, their response to the persecution was amazing. Acts 5:41 says, "And they departed from the presence of the council, rejoicing that they were counted worthy to suffer shame for his name." They were able to take a licking and keep on ticking.

We shouldn't mind suffering for the One who saved our souls. Our suffering is nothing in comparison to His suffering. Yes, many have died like He died. There is still no comparison. The reason those deaths cannot compare is based on what Jesus gave up to die. No one has ever given up as much as He did. He left His heavenly throne of perfection to come and dwell in a sin-sick world. He came for the purpose of dying so that we could one day live. My grandmother used to say, "He didn't have to do it, but He did and

I'm thankful." Therefore, if I am allowed to suffer for His sake, I should consider it an honor.

Courage to Expect Struggling (30)

Paul says, "Having the same conflict which ye saw in me, and now hear to be in me" (1:30). Paul was qualified to write these words to the family of faith. He was not like some "experts" who attempt to deal with a subject or problem they have never experienced themselves. As Paul wrote this information, he spoke from experience. When the Philippians read the letter, they could testify to his experience. The members of this Philippian congregation would know that Paul was a living witness, particularly the jailer who had put ointment on Paul's back made raw by the lashes he received before being thrown in jail. They saw it.

Paul wanted them to know that it hadn't stopped. His imprisonment had not been a bed of roses. He was still being persecuted for righteousness' sake. He wanted them to know that the information they had heard about his deplorable living conditions were true. Although he had witnessed persecution—and was witnessing it at the time of writing the letter—he considered it an honor and privilege to suffer for His sake.

Chapter 4

I Am My Brother's Keeper!

Philippians 2:1–11

The Relative Message
    The Supreme Facilitator
    The Supernatural Force
    The Sympathy Factor
The Right Method
    The Happy Preacher
    The Harmonious People
    The Harmful Plan
    The Haughty Path
    The Humility Principle
    The Helpful Person
The Role Model
    His Divine Position
    His Divine Place
    His Divine Prerogative
The Real Ministry
    The Perfect Performance
    The Primary Purpose
    The Planned Procedure
    The Providential Promotion
    The Powerful Position

The Relative Message (2:1)

The Supreme Facilitator (1a)

Paul says, "If there be therefore any consolation in Christ, if any comfort of love . . ." (2:1a). In the first few verses of this chapter, Paul deals with the subject of Christian relationships. He was aware of the unnecessary squabbling in the church at Philippi. Therefore, he began and built his case on a solid foundation for all believers. He starts with the common denominator that exists in the life of all Christians—Jesus Christ. He used two beautiful terms to describe the importance of incorporating the ways of the Supreme Facilitator. The first is *paraklesis*, the Greek word for "consolation" that means "to walk alongside" or "to draw alongside of one." The other word is *paramuthion*, translated "comfort." This particular word is found only in this verse of Scripture. It is a word that means "incentive" or "something that stimulates."

Paul wanted his friends to look to Jesus as they dealt with their relationships with one another. They needed to think about the consolation and comfort offered to all by Jesus Christ who was to serve as their incentive to love their fellowman. If anyone needed a reason to love his brothers and sisters, Paul gives it to them. Jesus is the reason. As consolers, the word implies that we should be there to help others. This is what the life of Jesus Christ was all about. He came to assist us when we were unable to do it for ourselves. If He had decided to assist only the deserving, He wouldn't have helped anyone since no one deserved the help that He offered.

When we have an incentive like Jesus Christ, we really don't need anything else to stimulate us to love one another and treat each other right. When I think about how Jesus loves me in spite of myself, I can't help but to love others. Not one of us deserves His love, but He loves us anyway. Some of us are not the most likeable people in this world but He still loves us. Let's use our Lord and Savior Jesus Christ as the incentive to love each other.

The Supernatural Force (1b)

Next, Paul says, ". . . If any fellowship of the Spirit . . ." (2:1b). If the incentive of Jesus Christ didn't give the Philippians the charge they needed, Paul now refers to the power of God that dwells in each believer. Don't allow the word "if" to confuse you in this verse.

Paul does not doubt the spiritual status of the believers to whom he wrote this letter. He believes that they are saved, sanctified, and filled with the Holy Ghost. Therefore, when he uses the word "if" in the verse, he is actually saying, "Since this is the case." Since the Holy Spirit dwelt in the hearts of the believers in Philippi, they had the power they needed to get along with one another.

There are several reasons why the Holy Spirit dwells in the believer's life. First, He *seals us*. He seals us until that day of redemption. This is why we cannot lose our salvation. If we were able to lose it, that would be suggesting that the Holy Spirit cannot do His job. The Holy Spirit *sanctifies us*. He helps us put our positional sanctification into practice. Also, the Holy Spirit *strengthens us* to do what we cannot do on our own. When He strengthens us, we find ourselves able to take more from others than we used to be able to withstand. You remember those days when all someone had to do was look at you the wrong way and you felt compelled to give him a piece of your mind. Since you now have fellowship with the Holy Spirit, you can take more from people because you have peace of mind.

I realize someone reading this might be wondering, *If I haven't made it to that point in my Christian walk yet, does that mean that there is no fellowshipping with the Spirit?* Once again, I must remind you that if you have received Jesus Christ as Lord and Savior of your life, the Holy Spirit now dwells in or fellowships with you. The problem may be that you are not spending enough time in fellowship with Him. He is waiting to take over if you would only allow Him to do so.

One morning our middle son awakened early. He knew it was daybreak because he could see some sunlight coming through the closed blinds on his bedroom window. Although the sun was coming up, it was still dark in his room. He wanted to get up, but he could not reach the light switch, and he was afraid. After a few minutes, he realized that although he couldn't reach the light switch, he could reach the handle to open the blinds at the window. After turning the handle, the sunlight burst into the room and the whole room was bright. This is how the Holy Spirit works. Like the sun, He has risen but the blinds are closed. If you want to get rid of the darkness, open the blinds of your heart and let the Spirit shine in.

The Sympathy Factor (1c)

After dealing with the incentive of Jesus Christ and the fellowship of the Holy Spirit, Paul concludes Philippians 2:1, by saying, "... if any bowels and mercies." Paul appeals here to the natural ability of the people. There is heart and compassion in even the worst of us. Even the Scrooges of this world have some compassion and heart. The word "bowels" is a euphemism meaning the core of a man's being which at that time was considered the kidney. At that time, instead of saying you loved a person with your whole heart as we would today, you would say, "I loved him with my whole kidney." It implies that there is love on the inside. The term "mercies" deals with the outward expression of that love. Therefore, the "inward devotion" is seen in the "outward duties."

Paul has covered all the areas that would enable the church to fulfill his joy. In a sense, Paul was letting them know in advance that what he was about to command them to do could be done because of what they were made of. They did not have any excuses not to do what was required of them.

The Right Method (2:2–4)

The Happy Preacher (2a)

Paul was already filled with joy. His relationship with the Lord caused that to happen. As a matter of fact, Paul could tell you that the joy of the Lord was his strength. He couldn't make it without this joy. However, Paul wanted the church to know that there were some things they could do to make him even happier. If they wanted to fulfill his joy, they had to behave in a way that was pleasing to the Lord. They could do some spiritual things to cause that cup of joy to continue overflowing. There is nothing more pleasing to a preacher or teacher of the gospel than seeing the life of a believer transformed as a result of the preaching and teaching. It is painful for the preacher to teach truth but never see people applying that truth to their lives.

It has always been impressive to me to hear people quote Scripture. I know people who can rattle off verses of Scriptures like reciting the alphabet or counting numbers. As impressive as that is to me, it depresses me to see those same people living in a way that does not support those recited verses. As a preacher of the gospel,

I am happy when I see the people of God applying the gospel to their lives.

The Harmonious People (2b)

Paul addresses the topic of unity again in this letter. If they wanted to fulfill his joy, they had to make sure they were unified. Once again, Paul dealt with a very sensitive situation that had developed in the church at Philippi. He knew that there was some friction between some of the members. Friction always leads to fractions. When friction exists between individuals, those individuals will try to get other people to support them. Paul says, ". . . that ye be like-minded, having the same love, being of one accord, of one mind" (2:2b). Paul then deals with three aspects of the spiritual walk that lead to the street of harmony.

First, we have the *shared beliefs*. He informs the church that they cannot walk harmoniously without being like-minded and without having one mind. For one to be like-minded means "to mind or think on the same things" or "to think alike." In the book of Acts, Luke wrote, "And they continued steadfastly in the apostles' doctrine and fellowship, and in breaking of bread, and in prayers. . . . And all that believed were together, and had all things common" (Acts 2:42, 44). You cannot have harmony in a congregation when the doctrines and creeds differ among the people in it. Every church should have a strong foundation built solely on the Word of God. When these beliefs are common among the members of the congregation, they have their minds focused on the same things.

This is why it is important for churches to have strong teaching ministries operating in the local assembly. It is a blessing to see so many churches filled to capacity on Sunday mornings. It is great to see people gathering for musicals and food fellowships. But where are those people when the Bible study classes are offered? Where are they when the church school lesson is being taught? We need to make sure that we are on the same page biblically if there is going to be unity in the body of Christ.

Next, we have the *soothing balm*. Paul reminded the Philippian church of the importance of allowing the same love to exist in the congregation. There was dissension in the church at Philippi, and Paul was offering a spiritual medication that could resolve the problem as well as prevent the problems in the future. They needed to allow the love of God to exist in their hearts and flow out to all the people. They were not supposed to love one member more than another. The same love should exist toward all of the members. People get along with others when they know they are loved by others.

The hurting brother or sister who becomes a part of the fellowship can see how this soothing balm provides a boost. Before coming to Christ, they had been wounded by people in the world. Even after coming to Christ, the same thing continues to happen to them in the world. The difference for the believer is that now there is a special place of escape. A believer should be able to find this love among the people of God. It is a love that you don't have to compete for. You don't have to have certain credentials to be a recipient of this love. You don't have to be a long-time member to receive this love. The same love is shown to all people.

According to Paul, the last requirement for Christian unity was that those in the church needed to become *soul brothers*. He told the believers at Philippi that they needed to be in one accord. The idea behind the term "one accord" is for believers to have their souls knitted together. Paul wanted them to become soul brothers. When you have the same love and the same creeds and doctrines that are biblically based, it causes you to be knitted together with others. It is a bond unlike any other. When souls are united, it is difficult to put a wedge between them.

The Harmful Plan (3a)

He says, "Let nothing be done through strife . . ." (2:3a). When things are done out of strife, it is an attempt to make someone else look bad. It is done out of spite. James 3:16 says, "For where envying and strife is, there is confusion and every evil work." It is an attempt to get even or to get the last lick or last word in. It is an attempt to inflict pain. Sometimes that pain is emotional, and other times it is emotional and physical. Why do you do what you do? Are you angry because of something that a person did to you and you have vowed to get even? This is a harmful plan even if you don't go through with it. The thought of evil is just as sinful. When we allow bitterness to dwell in us, it will eventually lead to some disaster. First you avoid speaking to a person. Next, you try to avoid sitting near that person. Then you will try to turn others against the person because you have a problem with the person.

Before long, a verbal fight takes place. In some cases, a physical confrontation occurs.

I remember a fight that took place in the parking lot of the church when I was growing up. As a child, I couldn't believe that these two women were fighting in the church parking lot. I saw the action blow by blow as I sat in the car waiting for my dad to finish assisting in the finance room. I could not believe that these two grown "Christians" were fighting. During a church meeting the following week, the women had to come before the church and confess and repent of their sins. Although children were not permitted to attend this meeting, the pastor asked my parents to bring me since witnessing the fight had had such a negative affect in my life. I had been devastated over the behavior of these grown women. I can't remember all the details of the meeting that night, but I do remember one thing that happened. Before it was over, the two women were in front of the church laughing because they couldn't remember how it all started since it had happened so long ago.

Paul knew that something like this could happen in the church at Philippi. If we fail to deal with the contentious spirits that rise in the church, years can cause the situation to worsen. It is like a weed that grows with the grass. If you simply mow over it, the weed will grow taller next time. As a matter of fact, the pieces of weed cut with the mower end up planted in other areas of the yard. Weeds will start growing everywhere.

The Haughty Path (3a)

He says that we should not allow anything to be done for "vainglory." Are you trying to get others to notice you? Are you looking for recognition? When something is done out of vainglory, it is an attempt to make one's self look good. It is an attempt to boost one's ego. Paul says that we should not allow anything to be done for this ungodly reason. Having pride and a haughty spirit is dangerous. The Bible says, "Pride goeth before destruction, and a haughty spirit before a fall" (Prov. 16:18).

The Pharisees had a self-righteous approach to life. Jesus spoke against their ways with passion. In Luke 18, Jesus told the story of a Pharisee and publican who went to the temple to pray. When the Pharisee prayed, he said, ". . . God, I thank thee that I am not as other men are, extortioners, unjust, adulterers, or even as this publican. I fast twice in the week; I give tithes of all that I possess" (Luke 18:11–12). This Pharisee was on the path of haughtiness. Some of the scribes were the same as the Pharisees. Jesus warned, ". . . Beware of the scribes, which love to go in long clothing, and love salutations in the market places, and the chief seats in the synagogues, and the uppermost rooms at feasts . . . these shall receive greater damnation" (Mark 12:38–40). Life was all about them and no one else. They traveled on the haughty path.

If you find yourself focusing on self and looking down on others, you are on the same path. If you are trying to get all that you can, while you can, and stepping on others to get it, you are on the haughty path. If you are always boasting about your accomplishments and achievements, you're on this path. None of us has bragging rights. What we have, God gave us. What we know, God taught us. Whoever we are, God made us. Where we are going, God will have to take us.

The Humility Principle (3b)

He says, ". . . In lowliness of mind let each esteem other better than themselves" (2:3b). When Paul speaks of esteeming others better than ourselves, he is not speaking of superiority vs. inferiority. He was not saying that we should consider everyone else to be more qualified or gifted than we are. He is dealing with the fact that everyone in the family of faith is gifted just as everyone else is. He is dealing with the way we should treat each other. The opposite of a haughty spirit is the spirit of humility. The Bible says, "Better it is to be of an humble spirit with the lowly, than to divide the spoil with the proud" (Prov. 16:19).

The humility principle says, "I will treat others the way I want to be treated." The humility principle says, "I will not look down on others, but will do all that I can to lift them up." The humility principle focuses in on being a servant rather than on being someone superior to others. Every person in the body of Christ is just as valuable as every other member is. Humble service causes harmony to exist in the church.

One day while the disciples were traveling with Jesus, a debate about who was considered the greatest among the group evolved (Mark 9:33–34). They wanted to know whom Jesus would select as His second man in charge. I am sure the guys started saying different things that they thought qualified them. Peter, James and John probably said they were the most qualified for special positions because they participated in more special activities with the Master. Matthew probably thought he deserved a special seat because he gave up more than the others did to serve Jesus. Jesus responded by saying, ". . . If any man desire to be first, the same shall be last of all, and servant of all" (Mark 9:35). They were viewing the subject of greatness from the world's perspective. In Matthew, Jesus said, "But it shall not be so among you, but whosoever will be great among you, let him be your minister, and whosoever will be chief among you, let him be your servant" (Matt. 20:26–27). From God's perspective, it requires a heart of service to really be considered as someone special in the kingdom.

The Helpful Person (4)

He also says, "Look not every man on his own things, but every man also on the things of others" (2:4). When there is unity in the body of Christ, there are going to be people concerned about each other. As a family member, the believer is going to always be concerned about the other family members. Paul is basically saying, "As a Christian, don't just be concerned about yourself; watch out for your brothers and sisters in the faith." When a member of the family is hurting, the pain should be felt by the other members of the family. When there is a need, other believers should do what they can to help out.

In Galatians 6:9–10, Paul says,

> *And let us not be weary in well doing: for in due season we shall reap, if we faint not. As we have therefore opportunity, let us do good unto all men, especially unto them who are of the household of faith.*

When we are concerned about the welfare of others, God will be pleased. God desires for us to live selflessly rather than selfishly.

The Role Model (2:5–7)

Paul decided that it was time to present a role model for them to examine. He could not have selected a better example than our Lord and Savior Jesus Christ. Paul said, "Let this mind be in you, which was also in Christ Jesus" (2:5). When Paul used the word "mind," it is the Greek word *phroneo,* which means "to think of." Paul was saying that the believer needed to think as Christ thought. As we shall see, His thoughts were never selfish or self-centered.

His Divine Position (6)

Paul says, "Who, being in the form of God. . . ." (2:6a). One day when Jesus started to prepare His disciples for His death and departure, He said, "I am the way, the truth, and the life; no man cometh unto the Father, but by me" (John 14:6). After Jesus said this to His disciples, Philip wanted Jesus to show them the Father. In John 14:9, Jesus says, ". . . Have I been so long time with you, and yet hast thou not known me, Philip? He that hath seen me hath seen the Father; and how sayest thou then, Show us the Father?" Jesus told them that they had been walking with God all along. Jesus knew who He was all the time.

It is evident that Paul knew who Jesus was. He tells the church at Philippi that Jesus was God. When Paul uses the term "form," he is not referring to the outward appearance of Jesus Christ. His nature was God. Someone has said, "If you took the body of Jesus away and left the behavior, you would have God." I believe that when Jesus was transfigured in Matthew 17, His outward appearance matched His inward nature. The text says, "And [Jesus] was transfigured before them: and his face did shine as the sun, and his raiment was white as the light" (Matt. 17:2).

When Paul says that Jesus was "in the form of God," he used the term *morphe,* which means "essential form." Jesus was not similar to God; He was the very essence of God. Not only was He the essential form of God, He did not count it as a prize to be equal with God: ". . . [He] thought it not robbery to be equal with God" (2:6b). The word for "robbery" is *harpagmos,* which also means "prize." He didn't have to look at it as a prize because He was God from the beginning. A prize is something that you receive after some accomplishment. John said it best when he wrote, "In the beginning was the Word, and the Word was with God, and the Word was God. The same was in the beginning with God. All things were made by him; and without him was not anything made that was made" (John 1:1–3).

His Divine Place (7a)

Paul continued by saying, ". . . [He] thought it not robbery to be equal with God: but made himself of no reputation . . ." (2:6b–7a). Although He was God, He made himself of no reputation. Here, when Paul says, "made himself of no reputation," he used the Greek word *kenosis*, which means "emptied." This "divine emptying" does not mean He was empty of His divinity. Normally when we think of something being emptied, we picture something being diminished. For example, we think of a bucket being emptied of its content as becoming an empty bucket. In the case with Jesus, the emphasis should not be placed on the bucket but on the contents in the bucket. If you poured water from a bucket into a jug, you still have the same substance in a different container. Jesus did not drop the attributes or nature of God to become a man. Jesus deliberately chose to leave glory and dwell among us. He moved from the bucket to the jug. It was His prerogative to do this. He did not relinquish any of His divine attributes to do it.

He has always been God. As a matter of fact, when He arrived on earth, it was recorded that God was present on the earth. John says, ". . . And the Word was made flesh, and dwelt among us . . ." (John 1:14). He did not discontinue being the *logos*, or the Word; He just became flesh and dwelt among us. Matthew said, "Behold, a virgin shall be with child, and shall bring forth a son, and they shall call his name Emmanuel, which being interpreted is, God with us" (Matt. 1:23). He did not cease being God.

His Divine Prerogative (7b)

Not only did He make Himself of no reputation, Paul says, ". . . [He] took upon him the form of a servant, and was made in the likeness of men" (2:7b). The word "servant" in the Greek is *doulos*. Jesus left His position and place to become a servant of the Father on earth. He came to serve and to show us how to serve. He chose to become the bondservant of the Father. In the Greek, Paul says, *morphe theou; morphe doulos*. He was both the "essential form of God" and the "essential form of man." He was not part God and part man. He did not empty Himself of deity, but simply covered His deity with the flesh of humanity. Paul said that He "was made in the likeness of men." When God chose to add His finishing touch to creation, He said, ". . . Let us make man in our image; after our likeness . . ." (Gen. 1:26). He was both God and man. He was the *theos anthropos*.

He chose to leave the heavenly throne, cover His glory with humanity, and dwell in this sin-sick world. Why would Jesus choose to do this? It was His prerogative and I'm glad He did it. He voluntarily chose to do all of this for us. He "made himself of no reputation" and He "took on him the form of a servant" to open the door of the throne to us. He emptied His nature as God into the body or flesh of a man for our redemption. It was a voluntary choice to move from His heavenly haven to dwell among us.

The Real Ministry (2:8–11)

The Perfect Performance (8a)

Since Paul addressed the church at Philippi about humility, he decided to remind them of the humility of Jesus Christ who humbled Himself before God. Man was made for this purpose as well. Jesus Christ demonstrated before humanity what God required from all of us. All of His life, He concentrated on pleasing the Father. In John 8, Jesus said, "And he that sent me is with me: the father hath not left me alone; for I do always those things that please him" (John 8:29). On several occasions, the Father announced His pleasure with His Son. After Jesus was baptized by John, a voice from heaven declared, "This is my beloved Son, in whom I am well pleased" (Matt. 3:17). On the Mount of Transfiguration, the proclamation came again. The life of Jesus was one of humility. There were never any selfish motives connected to His behavior. He always humbled Himself to the will of the Father.

You cannot be effective in ministry without humbling yourself before God. When we humble ourselves before the Lord, we please Him. We were all created for this purpose. John says, "Thou art worthy, O Lord, to receive glory and honour and power: for thou hast created all things, and for thy pleasure they are and were created" (Rev. 4:11). Later on in this chapter of Philippians, Paul says, "For it is God which worketh in you both to will and do of his good pleasure" (Phil. 2:13). Our goal in life should be to do whatever it takes to please Him. For many, the goal of life is to please self. For some, it is to please others. If we seek to please God, we will not ignore self and others. As a matter of fact, we will treat ourselves and others right according to the will of our heavenly Father.

The Primary Purpose (8b)

Next, Paul reveals the primary reason for the Word becoming flesh and dwelling among us. Paul said that Jesus became obedient to death. His humility toward the Father was so great that He was even willing to submit to the will of the Father for Him to die on the cross. He was born to die. The primary purpose of deity clothing Himself in flesh was not just to come and dwell on the earth. While on earth, He healed the sick and raised the dead, but that was not the primary purpose behind His coming. He came to give His life as a ransom for many. In Matthew 20:28, it says, "Even as the Son of man came not to be ministered unto, but to minister, and to give his life a ransom for many."

The Planned Procedure (8c)

Paul continued, ". . . And became obedient unto death, even the death of the cross" (Philippians 2:8b). He became obedient to death. It was not just any kind of death, but a horrible death on the cross. This planned procedure of Providence explains the reason why it was difficult for many to accept Jesus as Messiah. Before Paul was converted, He also had difficulty accepting Jesus Christ as the One who could have been the fulfillment of their Messianic expectation. For Saul and others like him, they could have accepted everything about Christ except for His death on a cross. His death was not a big problem for them because David and others in the Old Testament had prophesied it would happen, but it was the method that was the roadblock.

In 1 Corinthians 1:23–24, Paul says, "But we preach Christ crucified, unto the Jews a stumbling block, and unto the Greeks foolishness; but unto them which are called, both Jews and Greeks, Christ the power of God, and the wisdom of God." The reason the Jews considered it a stumbling block can be found when you examine the meaning of the cross to them. This method of torture and execution used by the Romans to put Christ to death represented the most disgusting form of death. They based their disgust on Deuteronomy 21:22–23 which says, "And if a man have committed a sin worthy of death, and he be to be put to death, and thou hang him on a tree: his body shall not remain all night upon the tree, but thou shalt in any wise bury him that day; (for he that is hanged is accursed of

God). . . ." They could not accept their promised messiah as one who would die a death that was cursed of God in the Old Testament. Paul pointed back to this passage in Galatians 3:13.

After Paul's eyes were opened, the death of Jesus on the cross became the most important symbol of salvation. When we pause to examine what the Lord went through for us, we can't help but to appreciate our salvation more and more. Jesus was bruised, beaten and humiliated for us. When we think of this kind of death as being accursed by God, we should picture ourselves hanging on the cross. Jesus was not a sinner hanging on the cross. Jesus took the sins of humanity and hung them on the cross in our place. Isaiah 53:4–5 says, "Surely he hath borne our griefs, and carried our sorrows; yet we did esteem him stricken, smitten of God, and afflicted. But he was wounded for our transgressions, he was bruised for our iniquities. . . ."

His death on the cross is the most important symbol for the believer. It was His death on the cross that led to the shedding of blood for our transgressions. When we examine the birth, death, burial, and resurrection of Jesus, we must understand why the death is more significant than all of them. All of these events in Jesus' life are important, but the death stands out. The birth and resurrection of Jesus were not difficult for the Father. It was not difficult for the omnipotent Father to cause Jesus to be born in Bethlehem. When Jesus was resurrected on the third day, it was not difficult for the Father at all. It was the death of Jesus that was most difficult. When Jesus was dying on the cross, the Father had to turn from Him and let Him die. When Jesus cried out, "My God, my God, why hast thou forsaken me?" it was more than a fulfillment of the prophetic utterance of the psalmist in Psalm 22:1. It represented a time when God turned His face from our sins that were hanging on Jesus as He hung on the cross.

The Providential Promotion (9)

Paul says, "Wherefore God also hath highly exalted him, and given him a name which is above every name" (2:9). As noted earlier, the death of Jesus served as the ransom and perfect sacrifice for our sins. He died for us and His death paid the price for our redemption. However, we must not leave Him on the cross or in the grave.

He has risen and is alive and well! When He was resurrected from the grave, He came forth with all power of heaven and earth in His hands. In 1 Peter 3:22, Peter says, "Who is gone into heaven, and is on the right hand of God; angels and authorities and powers being made subject unto him." Jesus has returned to His rightful place and now sits on the right hand of the Father awaiting the time determined by the Father to return to the earth. In Ephesians 4:10, Paul said, "He that descended is the same also that ascended up far above all heavens, that he might fill all things." The One who died and descended to hell to take the keys of death and hell from Satan has been exalted far above the heavens.

Once again, we see Paul teaching a valuable lesson to us and to the saints in Philippi. The life of Jesus teaches us that the way up is the way down. There are times when the way to the top requires the believer to hit rock bottom. It is true that sometimes the believer's humility will lead to humiliation as it did for Jesus Christ. However, the Father will exalt the humble and faithful in due season. When God exalts a person, no one can pull that person down. When we attempt to exalt ourselves, we may climb up the prestigious ladder of power and success, but it is hard to stay there. Sometimes the fall from that ladder is painful. The fall is always faster than the climb. If God lifts you up, you don't have to worry about the fall.

Not only has He been exalted by the Father, He has been given a name above every name. The songwriter wrote, "There is a name I love to hear; I love to sing its worth. It sounds like music in mine ear, the sweetest name on earth. Oh, how I love Jesus . . . because He first loved me." There is saving power in that great name. Romans 10:13 says, "For whosoever shall call upon the name of the Lord shall be saved." Acts 4:12 adds, "Neither is there salvation in any other: for there is none other name under heaven given among men, whereby we must be saved."

There is healing power in that name. When Peter and John were on their way to pray, a crippled man at the temple gate asked for alms. Peter and John looked at him and he looked at them, and Peter replied, "Silver and gold have I none; but such as I have give I thee: In the name of Jesus Christ of Nazareth rise up and walk" (Acts 3:6). There is petitioning power in His name. Jesus said, "And whatsoever ye shall ask in my name, that will I do, that the Father may be glorified in the Son" (John 14:13).

The Powerful Position (10–11)

The exaltation of Jesus will eventually lead to everyone recognizing His promotion. Paul says, "That at the name of Jesus every knee should bow, of things in heaven, and things in earth, and things under the earth; and that every tongue should confess that Jesus Christ is Lord, to the glory of God the Father" (2:10–11). These verses are prophetic. The complete fulfillment of these verses has not come to pass. Currently, the heavenly host and those of us who believe in Him are bowing before Him and have confessed with our mouths. However, the text says that "everyone" will eventually bow and confess. This has not occurred, but the day will come when all will bow and confess.

Periodically, I will encounter someone on the road of evangelism who will say, "I don't believe in that Jesus and God stuff." My heart is saddened by the rejection of Christ. I am also saddened by their atheistic philosophy. However, one day, those people will acknowledge Him as Lord. I only hope that day comes for those persons before the second coming of Christ. If they continue to reject Him until then, they will still bow—but it will be too late to be saved.

Chapter 5

The Discipleship Program

Philippians 2:12–18

The Disciples' Deportment
    The Righteous Conduct
    The Report Card
    The Right Challenge
The Defined Duty
    The Dwelling of the Spirit
    The Desire of the Soul
    The Deeds of the Servant
The Distinct Difference
    The Parallel Sins
    The Professing Saints
    The Perverse Society
The Drafted Directions
    The Christian's Guide
    The Celebrating Guardian
    The Correct Gauge
The Delightful Deference
    The Sacrificial Possibility
    The Shouting Preacher
    The Shared Praise

The Disciples' Deportment (2:12)

The Righteous Conduct (12a)

Their behavior as a church was wonderful. Paul says, ". . . as ye have always obeyed. . . ." Their conduct grade was impressive. It is always great to hear someone say that the spiritual behavior of another believer has always been consistent. In Matthew 5:16, Jesus said, "Let your light so shine before men, that they may see your good works, and glorify your Father which is in heaven." The Philippians were trying to let their lights shine on a daily basis. When they were in public, they obeyed. When they were behind closed doors, they obeyed. Their obedience was continuous.

They did not have a convenient Christianity like those who only obey when they are in trouble. When some people get into trouble, they pull out their religious clothes. They think their temporary state of holiness will make the trouble go away. They soon learn that this temporary state of righteousness did not keep the consequences of their past behavior from catching up with them. Some obey only when they want something. These are the people who become righteous all of a sudden because they want something from God. They think if they suddenly act righteous, maybe they will get the job promotion or the pay increase. However, God knows it is just a temporary state and that once the job comes through, the person will start acting the same as he did in the past.

Some obey only when they think others are looking. These are the folks who appear very saint-like at church. When other church members are looking, they seem to be the epitome of what it means to be a Christian. However, if you lived in their homes or saw them when they were unaware, you would not believe they were the same people. When they know other church members are watching, every other phrase they utter is "Praise the Lord." But when they think there are no church members around to hear them, every other word is a profane word instead of words of praise.

The Report Card (12b)

Paul says, ". . . Ye have always obeyed, not as in my presence only, but now much more in my absence . . ." (12b). They not only obeyed in his presence. The report Paul received about them supported the fact that they also were behaving in his absence. When other believers from Asia visited Paul in prison, I am sure he asked them about his friends. They reported about the way the Spirit of God was working in the lives of his friends in Philippi. He had seen first hand how they were living like Christians should live. However, by the time this letter was written, it had been almost a decade since he had been with them. It was always wonderful to see that they were doing well spiritually. They received some good grades on their report card.

One day, I took my boys to the barbershop. We had to wait to get their haircuts because the shop was crowded. I decided to leave them in the shop while I went to the bank across the street. When I returned, they were sitting in the barbers' chairs getting their haircuts. As I was about to leave, a man approached me and said, "Sir, I know you don't know me but I just had to tell you this. I observed all of the children sitting in the barbershop and their behavior. I was so impressed with the behavior of your boys. Their behavior was so good that you would have thought you were sitting in there with them all of the time." I must admit that his words made me so proud. What kind of report would be given about your lifestyle? I realize that some of your brothers and sisters in the faith who worship with you would probably submit a good report. I am more concerned about the report that would come from others. What grade would you receive from your spouse, children, parents, co-workers, classmates, or neighbors?

The Right Challenge (12c)

In the latter part of verse 12, Paul says, ". . . work out your own salvation with fear and trembling." Their straight "A" report card was not a diploma. They had not graduated. They needed to work out their salvation with fear and trembling. Of course, they didn't have to work to earn their salvation because Jesus Christ had already worked that out. If Paul had told them to work to earn salvation, it would imply that some action of man is required in order to be saved. Salvation is a gift. Romans 5:18 says, "Therefore, as by the offence of one judgment came upon all men to condemnation; even so by the righteousness of one *the free gift* came upon all men unto justification of life." In Romans 6:23, Paul says, "For the wages of sin is death; but the gift of God is eternal life through Jesus Christ our Lord." The only thing we earned was the right to die for our transgressions. Salvation is a gift from God given to all who receive Jesus Christ as Lord and Savior.

Once salvation is received, it is then time for the believer to get busy working it out. Salvation begins the moment we confess with our mouths the Lord Jesus and believe in our hearts that God raised Him from the dead. But this is just the beginning. The phrase "work out" is the Greek word *katergazomai*. It means working through to the full completion. It is like giving a student a math equation and allowing him to work through the problem step by step to get the answer. We cannot become satisfied with merely accepting Christ as Savior and Lord. It should be the goal of every believer to allow Him to reign as Lord. This can only happen when we work it out to its completion. When Paul wrote to his son in the ministry, he said, ". . . Exercise thyself rather unto godliness" (1 Tim. 4:7). The word "exercise" comes from the Greek word *gumnos*, from which we get our word "gymnasium." When we exercise, we attempt to build up what is already there. You don't exercise to get muscles; the muscles are already there. Your exercise is designed to cause those muscles to develop more. You also work out or exercise to get rid of that which covers the muscles. As you work out, fat and cellulite begin to fall off. The muscles were always there, but they had become covered with extra stuff.

Paul told the Philippians to work out their own salvation with fear and trembling. When he spoke of fear and trembling, he was not telling them to be afraid of anything that man could do to them. Paul referred here to the seriousness of the work to be done. He was thinking about the fear of letting God down. When we fail to work out our salvation, God is disappointed. We want to please God in all that we do. If there is no attempt to do what He has called us to do, we should be afraid. As we live in this world, we should live in such a way that God receives glory instead of gloom.

The Defined Duty (2:13)

The Dwelling of the Spirit (13a)

In Philippians 2:13a, Paul says, "It is God which worketh in you. . . ." The reason we can work out our own salvation is because of the One working in us. God never tells us to do anything without equipping us with what we need in order to do it. He has given us His Holy

Spirit to help us accomplish the task. If the Holy Spirit did not indwell us, anoint us, and fill our lives, we could not perform the work. In Ephesians 3:20, Paul says, "Now unto him that is able to do exceeding abundantly above all that we ask or think, according to the power that worketh in us." There is no excuse for us not to do what He requires of us because He has given us the spiritual tools needed to be successful.

The Holy Spirit will help us in many ways. First of all, He *energizes* the believer. In this verse, Paul uses the Greek word *energo* for work, which means "to energize." The Holy Spirit gives us the power to do what it takes. He also *encourages* us. As we work out, the Holy Spirit is there telling us that we can do it. When obstacles come, He speaks to our hearts and encourages us to keep going. The Holy Spirit *enlightens* us. There are times when we don't know which way to go and the Holy Spirit will cause a passage of Scripture to surface in our minds that we have read or heard in the past. He causes the Word of God to lead us down the right path. Lastly, He *enthuses* us. God has no desire for us to work out with our lips stuck out in a pout. He desires for every believer to be enthused and excited about serving Him.

The Desire of the Soul (13b)

When the will is not in it, the person is really not in it. As the Holy Spirit resides in the soul of the believer, there is a desire flowing from the emotion to please God. In Isaiah 26:8, the prophet says, "Yea, in the way of thy judgments, O Lord, have we waited for thee; the desire of our soul is to thy name, and to the remembrance of thee." The depth of the desire is contingent on the amount of control we have given the Holy Spirit. In other words, the more we walk in the Spirit, the more we will desire to live in the Spirit.

The Holy Spirit has planted the desire in all believers. It is up to us to water and fertilize the desire. Every time we study the Word of God, we are pouring some spiritual fertilizer on the desire. When we pray, we are watering the desire. If you fail to have a strong Bible study plan and a serious prayer life, don't expect the desire to grow and blossom. As a matter of fact, when we refuse to spend time in prayer and studying His Word, we are watering and fertilizing the flesh. The desires of the flesh will overrule the desires of the soul. The more we become filled with the Spirit, the more we will discover that our wills are beginning to interlock with His will.

The Deeds of the Servant (13c)

Paul says, "For it is God which worketh in you both to will and to do of his good pleasure." Desire without duty is dangerous. The Holy Spirit plants that desire in the soul, and it is up to the believer to act on it. Paul wanted the Philippians to know that a house full of people with good intentions was not sufficient. We must allow the deeds to accompany the desires of the soul. God does not want to hear any of us say, "Well, Lord, I desired to please You, but something always prevented me from doing it." As He works in us and gives us the desire, He looks for us to take care of the duty.

You will never find fulfillment in life until you discover that you were made for God's pleasure. Life should be about pleasing our maker. Solomon learned this lesson late in life. After trying some of everything to be satisfied in life, he discovered that he had been traveling down the wrong paths. At the end of the book of Ecclesiastes, Solomon said, "Let us hear the conclusion of the whole matter: Fear God, and keep his commandments: for this is the whole duty of man" (Eccles. 12:13).

The Distinct Difference (2:14–15)

The Parallel Sins (14)

Once again, Paul touches on an issue that he knew was taking place in the church at Philippi. He says, "Do all things without murmurings and disputings" (2:14). The word murmuring comes from a Greek word that means "to mutter, to complain, or to grumble." The word disputing comes from a Greek word that means "to oppose or to question." Grumbling or murmuring are outward expressions that grow out of the inward spirit of opposition or questioning. Disputing is not the same as disagreeing. If that were the case, some of the comments made by Paul in his letters would have been considered disputing or grumbling.

There is a major difference between Christians who have a dispute about an issue and Christians who disagree over an issue. If someone disputes something, it usually leads to *cutting criticism*. When one disagrees, it usually leads to *constructive criticism*. The cutting criticism from the grumbler is usually accompanied by *condemnation*. When there is constructive criticism from the one who disagrees, it is usually accompanied with *compliments*. Paul was challenging this body of believers to function without complaining and disputing. As believers, we should deal with issues without murmuring or disputing.

If there is any group in the Bible known for their murmuring, it would be the children of Israel. They complained when Moses arrived in Egypt right after their workload was increased. They complained at the Red Sea when they saw Pharaoh's army coming. They complained of thirst, and once they arrived at Marah, they complained of the water's bitterness. When they became hungry in the wilderness, they complained about not having food. When Moses stayed on the Mount of God for too long, they complained. When Caleb and Joshua came back ready to enter the land of promise, they complained because of the giants in the land. They were always complaining. Moses had to inform them that their complaints against him were really complaints against God. "And Moses said, This shall be, when the Lord shall give you in the evening flesh to eat, . . . for that the Lord heareth your murmurings which ye murmur against him: and what are we? Your murmurings are not against us, but against the Lord" (Exod. 16:8).

When we allow the Holy Spirit to work in us and through us, we can deal with all issues in a way that is pleasing to the Lord. When we murmur and grumble, we are not allowing the Spirit to do His perfect work in our lives. Murmuring is destructive, not only to the one being murmured against, but also to the one doing the murmuring. In Paul's letter to the Corinthians, he started listing the sins of the children of Israel and he reminded the church that we have received this information to learn from their mistakes. 1 Corinthians 10:10 says, "Neither murmur ye, as some of them also murmured, and were destroyed of the destroyer."

The Professing Saints (15a)

In Philippians 2:15a, Paul says, "That ye may be blameless and harmless, the sons of God, without rebuke. . . ." Paul used three interesting terms in this verse. For our word blameless, he used the Greek term *amemptos*, which means "without reproach." Then he used the Greek term *akeraios*, meaning "guileless, pure, unmixed, or sincere"—harmless. The word Paul used for without rebuke is *amometos*, which means "without blemish." The professing Christian should live above reproach, be sincere, and seek to have an unblemished life. Our goal as believers should be to become harmless and blameless children of God without rebuke.

Once again, I sense the need to remind you that God never expects us to do or become anything that He does not equip us with the power to accomplish it. The reason the Son of God did not come and go directly to the cross of Calvary was to teach us how we should live. He lived a sincere life above reproach and without blemish to show us that it could be done. Jesus had to deal with temptations just like we do. The Bible says, "For in that he himself hath suffered being tempted, he is able to succour [help] them that are tempted" (Heb. 2:18). He can identify with our temptations because He has been there. He was tempted but He did not give in.

The cowardly way out of this is to say, "Well, I am not God and man. I'm just human." That excuse will not work for several reasons. First of all, although He was God and man, He did not rely on His deity to live above reproach. He stayed focused on the Father's will for His life to win the battle over temptations. Another reason the excuse will not work is because of what Paul wrote to the church at Corinth: "There hath no temptation taken you but such as is common to man: but God is faithful, who will not suffer you to be tempted above that ye are able; but will with the temptation also make a way to escape, that ye may be able to bear it" (1 Cor. 10:13). When we yield to the temptation, it is because we chose to do it and not because we had to do it. The door of escape was open for us to exit. It doesn't matter what side of the tracks you were born on as long as you have been born-again. As believers, we must live in a manner that is becoming of God's children. As sons of God, we have a family image to project and protect. We also have a Big Brother willing to show us the way.

The Perverse Society (15b)

Paul reminds the Philippians of the kind of society in which they lived. He says, "That ye may be blameless . . . in the midst of a crooked and perverse nation, among whom ye shine as lights in the world" (2:15). It is difficult to be a witness to the world when believers act just like those in the world. There should be some distinct differences between the Christian and the unbeliever. The believer is told to be different in three particular areas.

First, the believer is to *walk straight in a crooked world*. The Greek word *skolias*, translated crooked, means "curvaceous or bent." We get the word scoliosis, a medical term that deals with the curvature of the spine, from this word. I love the story of Paul when he was converted. He was traveling on the crooked and winding road to Damascus. After encountering Christ on that road, he was sent to Straight Street. After you have been saved on the crooked road of life, you need to get on the straight street. We live in a world that is bent out of shape by the sins of humanity. No matter how crooked the world becomes, we must commit to walking the straight and narrow.

One of the ways to take a sobriety test is to be able to walk a straight line. When a person is unable to walk the straight line, it is usually a sign of intoxication. There are too many people in this world intoxicated by sin that are not able to walk the straight line of truth.

Next, Paul reminds the Philippians that the believer is to *live holy in an X-rated environment*. The world in which we live is perverse and pornographic. These things are done privately and publicly without remorse. A perverse environment is produced by a perverse people. Some are being perverse under cover as well as under the covers. We find this perversion in all walks of life from the preacher to the politician. The Bible teaches that those things done in the dark will come to the light. Proverbs 10:9 says, "He that walketh uprightly walketh surely: but he that perverteth his ways shall be known." The righteous man is safe, but the perverse man will be revealed.

Perversion is no longer a hidden sinful act of humanity. There was a time when you did not have to worry about sitting down as a family and watching television during the prime-time hours. Now, you have to preview the shows before you can call the family in. Talk shows have high ratings because of their desire to please the perverse people who have created this X-rated environment in which we live. Commercials sell their products by using half-dressed actors and actresses to promote it. Pornographic material can be found in the local market or on the home computer.

Lastly, the believer is to *shine in the midst of a dark society*. We live in a world of darkness because the prince of darkness is in control. In Matthew Jesus says, "Ye are the light of the world. . . . Let your light so shine before men, that they may see your good works, and glorify your Father which is in heaven" (Matt. 5:14a, 16). As lights in the midst of darkness, our behavior should be different from those who are living in darkness. Although the world is dark, our spiritual glow should dispel some of the darkness. As we shine, we may be able to lead someone out of darkness and into the marvelous light.

The Drafted Directions (2:16)

The Christian's Guide (16a)

Philippians 2:16a says, "Holding forth the word of life. . . ." As believers, we have been commanded to hold forth the word of life in this crooked, perverse and dark society. We should hold it forth because we ourselves cannot see our way without it. It is the roadmap or guide for the believer. It should always be before us as our guide. The Psalmist says, "Thy word is a lamp unto my feet, and a light unto my path" (Psa. 119:105). It should be held up so that we can see where we are going as well as show others how we got there.

The Word of God causes us to have life. The reason we have eternal life is because we heard the Word. The Bible says, "So then faith cometh by hearing, and hearing by the Word of God" (Rom. 10:17). Jesus came that we might have life and have it more abundantly. The abundant life comes when we hold forth the word of life. When the principles and precepts are put into practice, we really learn how to live. Have you ever read something in a book and tried to apply it to your own situation, only to discover that it wouldn't work for you? The book could have been written by a genius. It just didn't work for you. However, there is a book—and it is on the bestseller list—called the Bible. I guarantee that the application of the instructions will work for you.

The Celebrating Guardian (16b)

As you read this letter to the Philippians, it is evident that Paul viewed himself as their spiritual guardian. From the first day he arrived in their city, a unique relationship began. He saw them move from spiritual infancy to spiritual adulthood. He had seen them weaned from drinking milk and now able to eat meat. He views this body of believers as a special group God has given him charge over. The intimacy of the letter sounds like a parent writing his children. Paul says, ". . . That I may rejoice in the day of Christ . . ." (2:16b). On that day, he was looking forward to celebrating over the fact that many lives had been converted because of the gospel seeds he planted in Philippi years ago. In Philippians 4, Paul referred to this body of believers as his "joy and crown." He was looking forward to seeing all of the Philippian converts in glory when the rapture of the church occurs.

The Correct Gauge (16c)

For Paul, ministry was all about running the race and laboring in the vineyard. He knew what he had been called to do, and he wanted to make sure that none of it was done in vain. He had invested time, sweat, and tears as a missionary. He had been beaten, shipwrecked, jailed, snake-bitten, and ridiculed. He did not want all of this to be something he had done in vain. In his heart, he knew that it was all worth it. He just wanted the Philippians to do all that they could to make sure they were anchored in the faith. At the Judgment Seat of Christ, he wanted to receive an extra star in his crown for being faithful to the calling of Christ.

The measuring tape for the believer is the race run and the work done. If you want to measure how far you have run in the race, don't add up the number of times you went to church. Don't look at the amount of money you gave to worthwhile causes. Don't count up the number of auxiliaries you were involved in. What have you done to cause others to get on board the gospel ship? The race and the work started at conversion. How well are you doing now? Are souls being saved as a result of your running in the race? Are people being helped as a result of your efforts?

The Delightful Deference (2:17–18)

The Sacrificial Possibility (17a)

Paul knew what was at stake by being in prison. He did not want to keep any of the possibilities away from his friends. He had already discussed his desire to come again and see them. However, there was another possible outcome for this servant of God. It was possible that his fate included becoming one of the martyrs of the faith. He says, "If I be offered upon the sacrifice and service of your faith . . ." (2:17a). Paul was determined to be faithful to his calling no matter what the outcome meant for him.

The imagery projected by Paul in this verse stems from a practice of the Old Testament times. Whenever a person offered a sacrifice on the altar of the Lord, he would pour wine on the burnt sacrifice (Numbers 15:5–10). The pouring of the wine on the burnt offering was called libation. As the worshiper poured the wine from the cup on to the hot altar, the libation would go up in a puff of smoke. This concluded the sacrificial time of worship for the worshiper.

Paul knew it was possible that his blood would serve as the substance for the libation. In the past, his blood had flowed as a result of being persecuted for righteousness' sake. When he was whipped with many lashes in Philippi, the blood flowing down his back was the substance for the libation. Time after time, he suffered for the cause of Christ. In the future for Paul, the substance for the libation would flow from Nero's chopping block. For Paul, if the service of sharing the gospel meant suffering and sacrifice, so be it. This was the least he could do for the One who had done so much more.

Most of us really don't understand what it means to be persecuted for righteousness' sake like the believers from the early periods of Christianity were. Many of them experienced physical pain and suffering for their faith. They were burned at stakes, tortured with burning tar, whipped, beheaded, and even crucified on crosses. They refused to deny the faith even in the face of possible sacrifice. Surely, if they could be faithful while facing such possibilities, we should be able to stand bold when opposition comes.

The Shouting Preacher (17b)

One would think that the emotional state of Paul at that time would have been one of depression at the thought of martyrdom. However, this is not the case at all. Let's look at the symbolism again that Paul uses in this verse. As the worshiper poured the wine on the sacrifice for the libation, he was not sad about it. In the Bible, wine is a symbol of joy and enthusiasm (Psa. 78:65; 104:15; Zech. 10:7). Paul says, ". . . I joy, and rejoice with you all" (2:17b). Paul is shouting at the thought of suffering for the cause of Christ.

Let me use my Holy Ghost filled imagination for a minute. I can almost picture this scene. When Paul is writing this letter, he receives word that they had possibly set a date for his trial. One of the guards, look at Paul and says, "Listen, I think you are a pretty nice guy and I want to give you some advice. You had better hurry and find someone to represent you because the last fellow without representation is no longer in need of representation. He got the ax!" Paul, with pen and paper in hand, tells his friends in Philippi about the possible sacrifice. He is chained to a guard while other guards are posted. As Paul begins to think and write about the possible sacrifice, the joy bells in his soul started ringing. All of a sudden, he shouts, "Hallelujah! Praise the Lord!" He may have stood up and cut a little step.

One day a young man in the congregation where I pastor came into my office and said, "Pastor, will you teach me how to always be happy like you?" I looked at him and asked him to explain what he meant. He said, "Pastor, I have been watching you and I am always amazed to see you so happy. When people say and do things that cause the average person to lose it, you seemingly don't allow it to rob you of your happiness."

I responded by saying, "Drew, you have confused happiness with joy. It is the joy of the Lord that causes me to act the same." When the joy of the Lord is your strength, you can shout in the midst of suffering. Since joy is part of the fruit of the Spirit, and since the Spirit always dwells within me, I don't have to worry about the circumstances of life stealing my joy.

The Shared Praise (18)

Have you ever found yourself worrying about other brothers or sisters in the Lord because of their suffering? I have on several occasions. I try to figure out what I am going to say to them when I visit them in the hospital or following the death of a loved one. There have been times when I have braced myself before entering only to walk in on a praise party going on. Instead of being down and depressed, they are often praising the Lord for His goodness. Paul said, "For the same cause also do ye joy, and rejoice with me" (2:18). In essence, Paul was saying, "I know you are worrying about me, but I want you to praise the Lord with me instead." Instead of worrying, he wanted them to worship. Instead of sighing, he wanted them shouting. Instead of pouting, he wanted them praising. Since they were partners in his bonds, they were to rejoice with him.

When he said, "For the same cause," there are two things inferred. First, it was possible that Paul would be offered "upon the sacrifice and service of your [their] faith" referred to in verse 17. Nevertheless, he wanted them to praise the Lord. They were not to allow the outcome of his situation to keep them from rejoicing in the Lord. He wanted them to know that since he was all right with it, they should celebrate with him. The other thing inferred here is the fact that they were in the same boat. They were not exempt from the same thing possibly happening to them. There was no guarantee that they would not be offered upon the sacrifice of their service. In any event, they were to have joy and rejoice.

In these verses, Paul has revealed the traits of an authentic disciple. In summary, he has dealt with the *exercise* of the believer and his need to work out his soul's salvation. He dealt with the *equipment* needed to have an effective work-out. If the person is saved, he has been equipped with the power of God. Paul addressed the *elusions* of the believer. Complaining and disputations can interrupt and interfere with the work-out. Next, he dealt with the *examples* that must be shown to a crooked, perverse and dark society. Next, he dealt with the Bible as their source of *enlightenment*. They needed to hold it forth. Lastly, he dealt with the *enthusiasm* of ministry that may lead to suffering.

Chapter 6

Ministers on the Mission Field

Philippians 2:19–30

The Special Student
    The Commissioned Servant
    The Church's State
    The Commendation Shared
    The Careful Selection
The Satisfactory Service
    The Proven Son
    The Personal Satisfaction
    The Prisoner's Suspense
The Suffering Saint
    The Description of His Service
    The Difficulty of His Stay
    The Deliverance from His Suffering
    The Discharge from His Services
    The Description of His Standing
    The Deliberateness of His Sacrifice

The Special Student (2:19–21)

The Commissioned Servant (19a)

In Philippians 2:19, Paul says, "I trust in the Lord Jesus to send Timotheus shortly unto you. . . ." As noted earlier, this is one of Paul's most intimate letters written to the churches. Paul had just finished addressing the lifestyle of the believer. He has told them not to grumble and dispute among themselves. He has instructed them not to be like the people in the dark, crooked and perverse world. He told them to hold forth the word and to possibly expect his life to end in sacrifice. After giving these words of instruction, he returned to the words of intimacy.

He tells them that he is going to send Timothy to check on them. Although this is not one of Paul's writings known as the pastoral epistles, we can't help but notice Paul taking a pastoral role. A true pastor plays the role of prophet and priest. As prophet, the pastor must preach sermons designed to create discomfort for those in their comfort zones. As priest, the pastor must also preach sermons that are designed to create comfort for those who are uncomfortable. The pastoral epistles of Paul operate from this angle. One moment, his words probably made them say, "Ouch, that hurt." The next moment, his words probably made them jump for joy.

Who was this young man named Timotheus that he is sending to the Philippians? It appears that his father, a Greek, died when Timothy was young because he was raised by his mother, Eunice and his grandmother, Lois. They were both strong Jewish-Christians committed to their faith, and reared Timothy in the fear and admonition of the Lord. When you examine the list of partners of Paul, Timothy is the most oft-mentioned. He is listed as a joint-sender of 2 Corinthians, Philippians, Colossians, First and Second Thessalonians, and Philemon. Timothy, whose name means "honored of God," appears on the scene in the second missionary journey when Paul went back to Lystra (Acts 16:1–3). Although Paul was now in prison, Timothy was still with him. Paul used him to check on the affairs of churches in his absence.

The Church's State (19b)

Why was Paul sending Timothy to check on his friends in Philippi? Paul's answer: ". . . That I also may be of good comfort, when I know your state" (2:19b). Paul was sending Timothy to check on their affairs so that he can be at ease. Paul had received reports from others about his friends in Philippi. This is evident by the contents of this letter and the issues Paul addressed in it. He was knowledgeable of their faith and their works. However, he still desired to know more. We don't know how long it had been since he received his last report. But when you love other people, you want to hear about their state of affairs as often as possible. Paul loved this body of believers. Although we really don't have any way of knowing if Timothy made this trip or not, the fact remains that Paul wanted to send him to check on them since he didn't know when (or if) he would be able to do it himself.

He also was concerned about the last report he had received about them. There were some problems in the church that concerned Paul. He had received the information about the friction between certain members. Although he addressed that problem in more detail later in this letter, he wanted to make sure they didn't decide to be simply readers of the letter and not doers. Paul knew that if they allowed the infractions to continue, it was going to affect their work in the ministry. Therefore, he wanted to send Timothy to make sure the church was traveling down the path of righteousness.

The Commendation Shared (20)

Paul says, "I have no man likeminded, who will naturally care for your state" (2:20). In essence, Paul was saying, "Since I can't come myself, I will send someone who is just like me." Paul was sending someone who had Christian attributes similar to his own. For Timothy, this was a wonderful compliment and commendation to receive from his mentor.

Paul revealed several things to us about, Timothy, his son in the ministry. He was a *gifted brother*. The Spirit of God was at work in his life. Paul had been able to witness firsthand the fruit and gifts of the Spirit operating in Timothy's life. When Paul wrote Timothy, he told him to stir up the gift. Paul also knew that he was a *genuine brother*. Paul had seen so many brothers pretending to be what they were not. They were hypocritical in their living. They were wolves in sheep's clothing. When Paul described them later, he says, "Whose end is destruction, whose God is their belly, and whose glory is in their shame, who mind earthly things" (Phil. 3:19). Timothy was not like them. He was genuine regarding his ministry. He did not want to bring any shame to the God of his life nor to his mentor.

Paul also knew that Timothy was a *godly brother*. Timothy was knowledgeable of the same Lord that ruled Paul's life. The light from the lighthouse was shining through his life. When looking at Timothy, one could see the image of God's Son. When your relationship is genuine and the Spirit of God controls you, people will see how godly you are.

The Careful Selection (21)

There were other ministers around that Paul could have sent. However, Paul knew he had to be very careful in his selection process. He could have sent someone else, but there was a concern connected to their motives. He says, "All seek their own, not the things which are Jesus Christ's" (2:21). The motto for these people was: "Life is all about me, myself, and I." But for the genuine minister, the motto is: "For me to live is Christ, and to die is gain" (Phil. 1:21). Paul knew that sending just anyone to them could have ended up hurting instead of helping. When people who are supposedly working on behalf of Christ ignore the things of Christ, there are several things happening that you should be aware of.

First, the person who does not mind the things of Christ is *selfish*. Although he may be involved in ministerial affairs, the purpose of his ministry is fame and fortune. He desires to make a name for himself. He desires to be the one known as the best preacher of preachers. If he cannot benefit from the event, he would rather not be a part of it. He elevates self over the Savior. Paul warned Timothy of this type when he said, "If any man teach otherwise, and consent not to wholesome words, even the words of our Lord Jesus Christ, and to the doctrine which is according to godliness . . . from such withdraw thyself" (1 Tim. 6:3–5).

Next, this person is *scandalous*. If the person does not mind the things of Christ, he will do all that he can to get what he can. Since he is selfish, he will do what it takes to bring about self-aggrandizement. He simply goes through the motions of ministry. In 2 Timothy 3:5–6, Paul says, "Having a form of godliness, but denying the power thereof: from such turn away. For of this sort are they which creep into houses, and lead captive silly women laden with sins, led away with divers lusts." He is the one who has a love for material gain. Paul addressed this type when he said, "For the love of money is the root of all evil: which while some coveted after, they have erred from the faith . . ." (1 Tim. 6:10).

He is selfish, scandalous and lastly, *shallow*. Don't expect to hear or see anything spiritually profound coming from him. He is more concerned about the sweet sound of the sermon rather than the spiritual substance of the sermon. When it comes to the Scriptures, he usually knows just enough to get by.

The Satisfactory Service (2:22-24)

The Proven Son (22a)

Not only did Paul know about Timothy, the saints at Philippi also knew he was gifted, godly, and genuine. Paul said, "Ye know the proof of him . . ." (2:22). In other words, Paul was saying, "You have seen his creeds match his deeds for yourself!" When Paul mentioned Timothy's name in the salutation, the Philippians knew who he was. They had watched Timothy in the presence of Paul and knew that he was sincere about his calling. They knew that Timothy lived by what he preached because they had watched him in the past. It is not difficult to receive someone when you know from personal experience that this person is a proven saint.

It wasn't hard for Paul to commend Timothy because the character of Timothy had already been proven and seen by the Philippians. When your character has been proven in the past, it will not be difficult for you to be accepted in the future. There were probably some new converts in the congregation who did not know this man that Paul was going to send in his place. They probably started asking some of the seasoned saints questions about his character. When they were asked, they did not hesitate to agree with Paul. It wasn't just because Paul said it, but it was due to their knowledge of this man of God.

There is something else implied here that we shouldn't overlook. When Paul said Timothy had proven himself to them, it revealed that Paul knew they had been watching him. We should remember that others are watching us. Their observation should lead to the revelation of our consecration. We never know when God is going to use us to minister to those who have been able to observe us in the past. If they have seen holy living in the past, it will not be difficult to minister to them when the need arises.

The Personal Satisfaction (22b)

In verse 10 of the tiny book of Philemon, Paul referred to Onesimus as his son. He often used the father-son analogy in reference to those he mentored spiritually (1 Tim. 1:2; 2 Tim. 1:2; Tit. 1:4).

Here in the book of Philippians, Paul had this to say about Timothy, ". . . As a son with the father, he hath served with me in the gospel" (Phil. 2:22). Paul was expressing his personal satisfaction with Timothy. First, he dealt with *the connection*. Timothy had been with Paul since the second missionary journey had started. The relationship had really developed into a father-son relationship. Earlier, Paul had described him as being likeminded. This means that Timothy had taken on the ways of his teacher.

When I was growing up in a small town in Arkansas, the Wesley boys could not get away with acting up away from home. There were eight of us, and every time someone saw us, they not only could call us by our first names, they knew we were one of Henry Wesley's boys or my grandfather's grandchildren. The reason they knew it was because all of us resembled our father and grandfather. We looked like them, and a lot of our mannerisms were just like theirs. The looks were inherited and a lot of the mannerisms were learned. The things inherited existed because the genes that were in our father and grandfather were also in us. The learned behavior was based on the years of observing them and duplicating certain behavior. The same "re*gene*ration" that had occurred in Paul's life had also occurred in Timothy's life. After being around his father in the ministry for years, a lot of the spiritual behavior of Paul had rubbed off on Timothy.

Next, Paul deals with *the commitment*. He used the word *douleuo*, which means "to minister as a bondservant." This level of commitment is rare. Timothy had become Paul's slave or servant. Whatever Paul needed to have done, Timothy made himself available to do it. "How could Timothy allow himself to become a servant of a man?" you ask. Well, we are not talking about a mere man. We are dealing with a man of God who was doing all that he could to turn the world upside down for Christ. One of the gifts evident in his life was the gift of helps. A person with this supernatural ability to assist is needed to help other gifted people accomplish the tasks assigned to their hands. The person with this gift is excited to do whatever he can to cause someone to be successful in carrying out his or her commitment to the Lord.

Lastly, he deals with *the cause*. Timothy's assignment was to serve Paul, but the One making the assignment was Jesus Christ. Paul said that Timothy had served him "in the gospel." It had all been done for the cause of Christ. Timothy was committed to God and to the man of God.

The Prisoner's Suspense (23–24)

Paul wanted to send Timothy because he did not know what was in store for his life. He needed to send his minister ahead, and if it was the will of God, he planned to come later. It appears from Paul's letters to Timothy that he may have witnessed freedom for a season. However, it was short-lived. Paul was not one to live in denial. He knew Satan was upset with him and the life-changing message that he preached. He knew it was just a matter of time before it would come to an end.

Although Paul was living in suspense, he did not allow that to keep him from taking care of spiritual business. When some people of God are living in suspense, they take a break from their spiritual responsibilities until they learn what the outcome will be. Even if our lives hang in the balances, ministry should never stop. While Paul waited to find out his destiny, he continued to write, worship, and witness.

The Suffering Saint (2:25–30)

The Description of His Service (25)

Paul says, "Yet I supposed it necessary to send to you Epaphroditus, my brother, and companion in labour, and fellowsoldier, but your messenger, and he that ministered to my wants" (2:25). This is the only passage in the Bible that mentions this brother. However, we can learn a lot about him from the last six verses of this chapter. As a matter of fact, this one verse speaks volumes for this otherwise unknown gospel giant. Paul deals with his *placement in the family*. Paul had just finished talking about his son and now he speaks about his brother. Epaphroditus was Paul's brother because they were both members of God's family. As children of God, they had a special relationship as brothers in the faith. Regardless of the race or nationality he represented, he was a brother in Christ. As children of God and brothers in Christ, Paul says, "And if children, then heirs; heirs of God, and joint-heirs with Christ . . ." (Rom. 8:17).

Next, he deals with his *partnership in the field*. Yes, the harvest was plentiful and the laborers were few, but this brother was listed among the few laborers. He didn't mind getting busy and doing his part of the work assigned by God. He was not a lazy Christian but a laboring Christian. He did not become a brother by his works, but after becoming a brother, he knew that there was work to be done. He was from Philippi and had been sent by the believers there with a gift for Paul. From the description of Epaphroditus, he was the type of person who might have approached the captain of the ship he traveled on to ask: "Captain, since it will take us a few days to travel to Rome, is it possible for me to conduct a Bible study class on board the ship?" He had probably witnessed to all of the passengers before they arrived in Rome.

Next, Paul deals with his *participation in the fight*. Paul described Epaphroditus as a fellow soldier. This man was not a wimp but a warrior for Jesus. He was decked out in his spiritual armor to take a stand against the wiles of the devil. Satan knows he cannot do anything about your placement in God's family. Once you give your life to Jesus Christ, you are saved forever, and nothing is able to separate you from the love of Christ. Although he cannot do anything about your placement in the family, he will try to do all that he can to prevent your laboring in the field. Isn't it interesting how obstacles always seem to surface when you are trying to lead a person to the Lord? Satan is the culprit behind all of these troubles. However, he cannot win because God has equipped us with what we need to deal with him.

Next, he deals with his *position in the faith*. When we read about this brother, many of us think that he had simply come to bring Paul the gift from the Philippians. However, the delivery of the package was only a small part of his mission. The phrase, "he that ministered," comes from the Greek word *leitourgos*, which means "one who serves in an office, a minister." The term Paul used for minister refers to a missionary. This title represents a calling and appointment to an office in the church. Paul had a preaching missionary in his presence. Listen, even the preacher needs someone to preach to him. When we look at a person like Paul, we sometimes elevate him to a level of sainthood that is out of order. Although he is a holy and an anointed man of God, he still needed to hear from another anointed man of God. Epaphroditus served as that man for Paul.

The Difficulty of His Stay (26)

Paul says of Epaphroditus: "He longed after you all, and was full of heaviness, because that ye had heard that he had been sick" (2:26). First, we have the *homesickness of the preacher*. This brother longed after his family of faith in Philippi. I have several friends who are involved in foreign mission. Sometimes they are in some remote area of this world for years. I pray for them because I can't even imagine how difficult it must be for them to be away from loved ones at home. When I miss a Sunday away from church, or when I am away in revival for a few days, I start missing my friends and family. The thought of being away from friends and family for months would be difficult for me. Epaphroditus was experiencing a serious case of homesickness.

Next, we have the *heaviness of the problem*. Here, we have the Greek word *ademoneo*, which means "full of anguish and distress, or depressed." "If he was as spiritual as you stated earlier, how can he be depressed?" you may ask. Well, it happens to the best of us. As a matter of fact, the only other time this word is used in the New Testament is when Jesus takes the members of the inner circle with Him to the Garden of Gethsemane. If it could happen to Jesus, I think it can happen to anyone.

Next, we have the *heartache of the people*. The reason he was homesick, heavy and hurting was because of the heartache of the people back home. Epaphroditus was not homesick and heavy because he had become tired of doing the spiritual things in Rome assigned to him. He enjoyed ministering to Paul. However, he knew they had heard that he was sick and were really concerned about him. He was concerned about the concern of others. This reminds me of the Lord's prayer in John 17 when Jesus poured out His heart to the God. Jesus knew that His departure was inevitable and He spent all of his time praying for the disciples instead of the cross in His path. He was more concerned about the disciples than He was about His own death.

The Deliverance from His Suffering (27)

Paul says, ". . . Indeed he was sick nigh unto death: but God had mercy on him; and not on him only, but on me also, lest I should have sorrow upon sorrow" (2:27). First, Paul deals with the *serious sickness*. The homesickness of Epaphroditus came after a serious bout with some physical ailment. While in Rome, he became gravely ill. We are not told what the sickness was or how long it lasted.

As believers, we are not exempt from the sufferings in this world. Epaphroditus was a strong Christian brother serving on the battlefield, and God permitted him to get sick. In other words, regardless of how spiritual you are, sometimes rebuking the sickness will not rid you of it. This spiritual soldier who served the Savior witnessed sickness. Although we don't know the sickness, whatever condition he had almost took his life.

Next, Paul reveals information about the *servant's survival*. Paul said that Epaphroditus almost died but God was merciful. He should have died but due to God's mercy, he survived. Paul was thankful to God for His divine intervention. I am sure that Paul prayed for him and laid hands on him, but this was not going to be the route of God's deliverance. God allowed him to get close to death before He delivered him. The fact is that this brother would have died if it had not been for the mercy of God. This event has a salvific ring to it, doesn't it? Epaphroditus was about to die, but God had mercy on him. We were already dead, but God had mercy on us. In Ephesians 2:1–6, Paul said, "And you hath he quickened, who were dead in trespasses and sins. . . . But God, who is rich in mercy, for his great love wherewith he loved us, even when we were dead in sins, hath quickened us together with Christ, (by grace ye are saved)."

Lastly, Paul talked about his *spared sorrow*. Paul realized that the mercy was not just for his sick brother, it was for him as well. God decided to spare Paul from additional sorrows. He'd already had many sorrows. He had to be chained to different guards every day. His trial date was taking forever to take place. He was in suspense and didn't know what would happen to him. His friend had become gravely ill. Yes, Paul had witnessed a lot of sorrows in his life. If his friend had died, it would have added to Paul's lengthy list of sorrows. God decided to show mercy to him and Epaphroditus. God knew that the death of Epaphroditus would have created more sorrow for Paul. Aren't you glad He knows just how much we can bear?

The Discharge from His Services (28)

Paul says, "I sent him therefore the more carefully, that, when ye see him again, ye may rejoice, and that I may be the less sorrowful"

(2:28). First, we have the *diligent decision*. When Paul uses the phrase "the more carefully," he is saying, "it is to be done with diligence and earnestness." Paul thought about it, and with diligence he sent him home. It was not easy for Paul to bid his friend farewell. He was going to miss seeing his friendly face every day and sharing the good news with each other. Paul also wanted his friends in Philippi to know that Epaphroditus was sent home and he was not AWOL. Instead of being selfish and keeping Epaphroditus with him, Paul told his friend that it would be best for him to return to Philippi.

Next, we have the *delighted disciples*. Paul knew what would happen when the word was out that Epaphroditus was coming home. They would be delighted and excited. They would organize a homecoming parade for the soldier. They would get a caravan to go down to the Port of Philippi to meet their friend and brother. Just seeing him walking off the boat would have caused their joy bells to ring. They probably would have held a special welcome-home fellowship at the church. They probably set up a revival featuring Epaphroditus as the speaker each night. They wanted to hear about his stay in Rome and about their spiritual guardian who was in jail.

Lastly, Paul talks about the *decreased distress*. Paul says that he was sending him back so that Epaphroditus would be less sorrowful. Paul is not saying that this brother had become a burden. This brother had been a blessing in Paul's life. He had helped to relieve some of Paul's burdens. When Paul speaks of becoming less sorrowful, he is dealing with the blessed relief that will come as a result of being able to send his friend home to the ones who had been concerned about him. Paul started to think about his friend almost dying without having an opportunity to go home to see his friends and family in Philippi. Now that his health had been restored, Paul did not want to waste any time getting his friend back home, just in case the illness recurred.

The Description of His Standing (29)

Paul says, "Receive him therefore in the Lord with all gladness; and hold such in reputation" (2:29). The phrase "in reputation" is the Greek word *entimos* and is translated "precious." Not only did Paul want them to receive Epaphroditus with gladness, he also wanted them to esteem him highly. Paul wanted them to know that he was a precious brother beloved. Paul wanted them to know exactly how blessed they were to have a precious man like Epaphroditus in their midst.

It is good when we take the time to compliment someone in the body of Christ. If anyone should speak kindly about another Christian, it should be another Christian. People in the world may call us everything but a child of God, but believers should share words that build others up rather than destroy them. In Ephesians 4:29, Paul says, "Let no corrupt communication proceed out of your mouth, but that which is good to the use of edifying, that it may minister grace unto the hearers."

The Deliberateness of His Sacrifice (30)

Paul concludes this chapter by saying, "Because for the work of Christ he was nigh unto death, not regarding his life, to supply your lack of service toward me" (2:30). First, we have the *consequences of the service*. Although we are not told what illness Epaphroditus had, we do know that his diligence in the work of Christ had led to it. From this information, we know that the sickness of Epaphroditus was not caused by anything he did wrong. I heard a minister preach from this passage years ago who claimed that Epaphroditus' sickness was probably a bleeding ulcerated stomach that had developed from worrying. We know that wasn't the case because of what this verse tells us. He did not get sick because of some bad habit he possessed. It was his devotion to the work of Christ that somehow had led to this sickness. As noted earlier, when you are working for the Lord, the devil will do what he can to prevent you from being successful. When you work for Christ, you should expect the devil to attack.

Next, we have the *commitment of the servant*. Yes, your involvement in ministry can lead to difficulties; however, we should remain committed to the cause. Paul used the Greek term, *parabouleuomai*, which means "disregarding or not concerned." Epaphroditus did not let the circumstances or consequences deter him from doing what he had been called to do. It sounds like Timothy and Epaphroditus had the same philosophy of Paul had expressed earlier: "For to me to live is Christ, and to die is gain" (Phil. 1:21). Epaphroditus' illness probably led to him being bedridden. However, I can imagine that he was still providing as much service as possible before this time arrived. He was committed to serving even while being sick.

For some believers, it doesn't take a whole lot for them to sit down on their calling. They don't have the determination and commitment required to stay faithful in spite of what happens.

Lastly, Paul deals with Epaphroditus as the *conduit of the saints*. Paul says, ". . . he was nigh unto death, not regarding his life, to supply your lack of service toward me" (2:30). When you first read that, it sounds as if Paul were complaining about the Philippians' lack of service. This is not what Paul is dealing with at all. Paul was very appreciative toward the Philippians for providing more assistance than all of the other churches. In this verse, Paul refers to the fact that Epaphroditus was selected as the one to represent all of them. Had it been possible for all of them to go to Rome, they would have been there. Instead, they decided to use the financial resources to help their mentor and friend who was in jail. Paul was saying, "Since you all could not afford to come, you allowed Epaphroditus to serve as a conduit of your generosity" Paul would have loved to have seen them all, but since he couldn't, their representative was the next best thing.

CHAPTER 7

Merited Favor:
When the Gains Outweigh the Losses

Philippians 3:1–11

The Reformed Requirements
    The Rejoicing Saints
    The Repetitious Style
    The Religious Scam
    The Right System
The Religious Rites
    Religious Righteousness
    Reserved Rights
    Ritualistic Rules
    Race Relations
The Regenerated Rebel
    The Assets of a Religion in Crisis
    The Availability of a Relationship with Christ
    The Absence of Righteousness through Ceremonies
The Redeemed Relationship
    The Correct Approach
    The Christian's Attire
    The Consuming Ambition
The Rejected Redeemer
    The Power of His Resurrection
    The Pain of His Rejection
    The Passion of His Redemption
    The Promise of His Reward

The Reformed Requirements (3:1–3)

The Rejoicing Saints (1a)

Paul deals with the overall theme of the letter again by telling the saints to rejoice. He says, "Finally, my brethren, rejoice in the Lord . . ." (3:1a). Although Paul used the term "finally" in this verse, he was really just getting his second wind. He still had a great deal to say to his friends. The first two chapters only represent half of what he had to say to them. The saints at Philippi would not respond to this phrase like some of us would respond. When some of us hear the preacher say "finally," or "in conclusion," we say to ourselves, "It's about time!" But for the Philippians, the longer the letter, the better. They missed Paul and wanted to hear as much as possible from him.

Once again, the theme of the letter surfaces. Paul tells his friends to rejoice in the Lord. When Epaphroditus arrived, Paul knew he probably started sharing information about Paul's condition as he was under house arrest in Rome. He probably revealed the details of how Paul was guarded twenty-four hours a day. He probably talked about Paul's being confined to his lodgings, handcuffed to one of the soldiers who guarded him in four-hour shifts. He probably told about Paul still waiting in suspense on his case to come up for hearing before the tribunal. This news had to be disheartening to the saints in Philippi. Therefore, Paul knew that he needed to encourage his friends as much as possible in this letter. Since he wanted his friends to sing instead of sigh, he repeatedly tells them to rejoice.

This was easier to say than to do. How did Paul expect them to rejoice, knowing that he was in prison? How could Paul expect them to rejoice after receiving the news that he was in suspense and did not know the outcome? Well, it is important to note that Paul did not tell them just to rejoice, he said, "Rejoice in the Lord." Although the situation may have been uncertain, the Savior remained the same. Although there was some bad news from Rome, the news of the Savior is always good news. When we learn how to rejoice in the Lord, it really doesn't matter what is happening in our lives. When we focus on the Savior rather the situations, we can rejoice.

The Repetitious Style (1b)

He made no apologies for repeating the information he had already shared with them before. He says, ". . . To write the same things to you, to me indeed is not grievous, but for you it is safe" (3:1b). Paul had not run out of new things to say to his friends. He made it clear that he was repeating or restating some things for their benefit. Paul realized that repeating and restating information would help them remember that information.

It is a known fact that the more you hear and see something, the easier it is to remember it. This is the system used with commercials advertising a product. When you hear a jingle about a product long enough, before long you start singing that jingle in your sleep. The same thing works with remembering God's Word. I had a friend in college who taught me a very important lesson about remembering the Scriptures. I was always impressed with his ability to recite passages from the Bible. One day, I found out his secret. Every morning, he would find a few verses of Scripture to recite over and over during the day. When people asked, "What's up, Jeff?" or "What's the word, Jeff?" he would recite those verses of Scripture. The more he recited it, the more it became etched in his mind. The repetition of the verses led to the remembering of those verses.

This is the same system God had told the Israelites to use on their children. Deuteronomy 6:7 says, "And thou shalt teach them diligently unto thy children, and shalt talk of them when thou sittest in thine house, and when thou walkest by the way, and when thou liest down, and when thou risest up." God wanted them to repeat His commandments as much and as often as possible. The more they repeated them, the more their children (and they themselves) would retain.

The Religious Scam (2)

Paul says, "Beware of dogs, beware of evil workers, beware of the concision" (3:2). He warned the Philippians to beware or look out for the scam artists that had wiggled their way into the congregation. First of all, he describes them as *righteous hounds*. Whenever the term dog is used in the Scriptures, it always is a negative or degrading term. Dogs were considered unclean animals that usually were seen roaming in packs. When Paul uses the term to warn the Philippians, he was dealing with a group who tried to insist that certain legalistic practices must take place before a person can become a member of the family of faith. For these Judaizers, salvation was all about what "thou shall and shall not do." Paul had already taught them that salvation was not about a bunch of rules, but about a beautiful relationship. Paul wanted the church to beware of these dogs and their barking and biting. Paul used this uncomplimentary term to warn the Philippians of their attempt to come in and devour the sheep.

Next, he described these scam artists as *religious hellions*. He tells the Philippian believers to watch out for the evil workers. Paul was not talking about evil people in the world. He was warning them about the evil workers that worshiped right there with them and had their names on the church roll. Paul used the Greek term *kakos*, which means "crooked, depraved, or bad," and is translated here as evil. In the house, there were crooked church members, depraved disciples, and some bad boys. It is possible that these false teachers were behaving like Christians in the church but that their lifestyles away from the church were evil. Their creeds didn't match their deeds. One day you see them living in the light and the next day you don't see them because they are hiding in the dark. Paul warned the Corinthians of these deceitful people when he said, "For such are false apostles, deceitful workers, . . . and no marvel; for Satan himself is transformed into an angel of light. Therefore, it is no great thing if his ministers also be transformed . . . whose end shall be according to their works" (2 Cor. 11:13–15).

Lastly, he described these scam artists as *ritualistic heathens*. Paul used the Greek term *katatome*, concision, to describe these false teachers in the church. This is the only place in the Scripture where the word is used. The verb form of the word concision is found twice in the Old Testament (Lev. 21:5; 1 Kings 18:28). The word deals with a heathen practice that involves the cutting of the flesh. The false teachers had come into the fellowship to try to reinstitute the religious practice of circumcision. They insisted that it was a requirement for people to be saved. Paul viewed this practice of requiring circumcision in order to be saved as being nothing more than the mutilation of the flesh. He wanted the Philippians to know that the new covenant produced through the shedding of the precious blood of the Lamb had rendered the Old Testament practice of circumcision null and void.

The Right System (3)

He says, "We are the circumcision, which worship God in the spirit, and rejoice in Christ Jesus, and have no confidence in the flesh" (3:3). In the Old Testament, all Jewish boys had to look forward to a painful practice after one week of existence. On the eighth day of life, the boy was circumcised in order to become aligned with the Abrahamic covenant (Gen. 17:10–14). Any adult converting to Judaism had to undergo the painful act of circumcision in order to be accepted. Later, the Mosaic covenant fell in line with Abrahamic covenant.

As time rolled on, the act of circumcision became a means of distinguishing between Jew and Gentile. Gentiles came to be regarded by the Jews as "the uncircumcision," implying that Gentiles were outside the circle of God's love. They used circumcision to boast about their relationship with Abraham, the father of the faith. In Romans, Paul revealed that it wasn't the circumcision of Abraham that saved him; it was his faith (Rom. 4:9–12). Due to this religious prejudice of the Jews, Paul had Timothy circumcised before allowing him to go with him on his missionary journeys (Acts 16:3).

But in this verse, Paul informed the family in Philippi that there was no need to be circumcised as the Judaizers insisted because they had already been circumcised. In Colossians Paul says, "And ye are complete in him, which is the head of all principality and power: in whom also ye are circumcised with the circumcision made without hands, in putting off the body of the sins of the flesh by the circumcision of Christ" (Col. 2:10–11). He expresses that the true worshiper is the one who has a circumcised heart and worships God in the Spirit without having confidence in the flesh. Paul wanted it understood that the cutting of the flesh could not save. The cross of Calvary removed the necessity of the Old Testament system and ushered in the right system.

The Religious Rites (3:4–6)

Religious Righteousness (4a)

Next, he addressed the righteousness obtained by doing things connected to the law. Paul says, "I might also have confidence in the flesh . . ." (3:4a). Paul continued his journey down the path of righteousness gained through human actions. When he speaks of confidence in the flesh, he is dealing with the attempt to earn God's favor through deeds of the flesh. In Romans 10:2–3, Paul said, "For I bear them record that they have a zeal of God, but not according to knowledge. For they being ignorant of God's righteousness, and going about to establish their own righteousness, have not submitted themselves unto the righteousness of God." All of the rituals, ceremonies, and celebrations were designed to elevate the Pharisees and other Jews above everyone else. Instead of becoming righteous in God's sight, the religious practices led to self-righteousness. In these verses, Paul was saying, "If I didn't know any better, I would have confidence in the flesh like others." Paul understood the problem of those trying to convince the Philippians of their practices. He understood the urge and desire to try and get others in line with this way of thinking. The reason he understood was because he had done the same thing in the past.

The main reason he had tried to destroy the church was because he did not believe in their preaching that Jesus Christ's death had broken down the walls that had prevented direct access to the Father. Before Paul received Jesus Christ and had his name changed from Saul to Paul, he could not accept these people who claimed to be connected to God the Father through His Son. Saul and others thought it was sinful for people to go around telling others that the Son of God had redeemed them back to the Father. For Saul and others, this was considered blasphemous. From his perspective, if they did not follow the Jewish custom of circumcision, they did not have the right to make these claims. Saul and others like him were to be considered the only ones who were religiously righteous.

Reserved Rights (4b)

Paul continues: ". . . If any other man thinketh that he hath whereof he might trust in the flesh, I more" (3:4b). He said he was qualified to say everything that he was saying because of his background. If anyone was deserving of a special place based on ceremonies and rituals, he believed he would have been first on the list. For years, before his conversion, Paul probably would have made the "Top Ten" list of Jews in Jerusalem. His religious résumé would have outweighed any of the Judaizers who were planting these deceptive principles in the church. This is why he could say, "I more."

Paul used a system of addressing the adversary that was similar to the way of Christ. On many occasions, Jesus had to let others know that He was more qualified to address an issue than they were. He simply spoke the truth and moved on to something else.

When they talked about Abraham's status over His, Jesus would reply, "Before Abraham was, I am" (John 8:58). This is the same approach Paul used here. He knew that as this letter was being read, those teaching these things would probably say, "He has some nerve calling us dogs and evil persons because we are telling the truth about the laws of God. Who does he think he is"? Paul was about to answer that question for them.

Ritualistic Rules (5a)

Some of the Judaizers were probably initiated into the Hebrew community as adults. They would have still had to go through the torturous rite of circumcision in order to be accepted. On the other hand, Paul had followed the rituals associated with the law and was circumcised on the eighth day. As the Abrahamic covenant required, the parents of Saul had him circumcised a week after he was born. This ritual made him a bona fide and branded member of the Hebrew religious family. Therefore, Paul could have boasted of being right from the beginning from a ritualistic perspective. Many of the Judaizers could not make such a claim.

Before the cross of Calvary, many Jews, including Jesus, were submissive to rules of the Abrahamic covenant. In Luke 2:21, we read, "And when eight days were accomplished for the circumcising of the child, his name was called JESUS, which was so named of the angel before he was conceived in the womb." Since Paul was well received and respected by the Philippians, I can imagine that the Judaizers used his circumcision as a means of arguing their point. When someone would question the Judaizers about the necessity of it, they would probably say, "Since Jesus and Paul were circumcised, there shouldn't be any more discussion on the matter." The part that they didn't want to address was the fact that when Jesus came and died on Calvary, all of the law was fulfilled.

Race Relations (5b-6)

Next, we have the *special claims*. Paul says, "Circumcised the eighth day, of the stock of Israel, of the tribe of Benjamin, an Hebrew of the Hebrews . . ." (3:5). He could boast about his affiliation with the stock of God's chosen people. The children of Israel have always had a special place in the heart of God. The relationship was so special that a covenant existed between God and them. Paul could also boast about the tribal unit that he came from. He could boast about his tribal affiliation as a Benjamite. The first king of Israel came from this tribe. He could also boast of the purity of his bloodline. He was a "Hebrew of the Hebrews." This phrase suggests that both parents were Jewish. There was not any mixed blood in him. His parents made sure he was rooted and grounded in the traditions of Jewish orthodoxy.

Next, he deals with the *sacred class*. Paul wanted the Judaizers to know that he was aware of the law and the observance of the law because he belonged to a sect that emphasized obedience to the law. He was connected to the special class of Jews called the Pharisees. The name means "separated ones." These Jews had their roots in a group of Hasidic Jews. The Hasidic Jews insisted on strict observance of the Jewish ritual laws. They believed in following the law as it was prescribed by a group known as the scribes. They did not like to mingle with other groups that did not observe the law as strictly as they observed it.

Next, he deals with the *suffering church*. He was known for his hatred of those who followed the Way. Before he met Christ, Paul was on a personal mission to put the church out of business. The infant church knew about his determination to destroy the church. As a matter of fact, when he was converted, Ananias, a disciple of Christ in Damascus, questioned God's command to him to pray for Saul and lay hands on him. Ananias was hesitant because he knew about Paul's threats against the church. The Lord had to remind Ananias that Paul was his chosen vessel (Acts 9:1–16).

Lastly, we have the *sincere commitment*. He says, ". . . Touching the righteousness which is in the law, blameless" (3:6b). Paul, as Saul, had believed that the only way to God was through the pharisaic practices that he believed in. In Galatians 1:13–14, Paul wrote, "For ye have heard of my conversation [manner of life] in time past in the Jews' religion, how that beyond measure I persecuted the church of God, and wasted it: and profited in the Jews' religion above many my equals in mine own nation, being more exceedingly zealous of the traditions of my fathers." Before his conversion, Paul had not thought of his persecution of the church as a sinful act. Instead, he thought his mission had been ordained by God since the church was claiming to have access to God by some way other than the law. He was sincere about keeping the law to the best of his ability. He did it all. He kept the Sabbath. He offered the sacrifices. He was committed to tithing and fasting. Whatever the law required, he tried to remain blameless. In other words, no one could accuse him of being a phony Jew.

The Regenerated Rebel (3:7–9a)

The Assets of a Religion in Crisis (7a)

Paul says, "What things were gain to me . . ." (7a). Paul was dealing with all of those religious accomplishments as a Jew that had been part of his past. Paul may have been blameless by doing what the law required, but being blameless did not equate to being righteous. It was impossible for righteousness to be obtained through keeping the law. Another problem for Paul and others like him was that they were trying to keep the commandments while waiting on the promised Messiah. He had already come and gone. In Galatians 2:16, Paul says, "Knowing that a man is not justified by the works of the law, but by the faith of Jesus Christ, . . . for by the works of the law shall no flesh be justified."

The practices of the Jews were not designed to be eternal. They were designed to take place until Jesus Christ came. When Jesus came and died for the sins of the world, the veil of the temple was split. This split symbolized that God had fulfilled the law through the shedding of the blood of His Son. Although the Jewish practices were commanded by God, the continuing practice of them after the resurrection of Christ was unnecessary. In Colossians 2:16–17, Paul wrote, "Let no man therefore judge you in meat, or in drink, or in respect of an holyday, or of the new moon, or of the sabbath days; which are a shadow of things to come; but the body is of Christ." Why consider the shadow of the Messianic hope as a gain, when you can have the body?

The Availability of a Relationship with Christ (7b–8)

Paul says, "Yea doubtless, and I count all things but loss for the excellency of the knowledge of Christ Jesus my Lord: for whom I have suffered the loss of all things, and do count them but dung, that I may win Christ" (3:8). Paul had been on a path that would have one day placed him in one of the highest positions a Jew could achieve. One day, he could have become the head of the Sanhedrin

Council. He had received his training by studying under Gamaliel, one of the greatest Jewish teachers of that era. He had a blameless track record when it came to keeping the rituals associated with the law. One day, he could have become the chief Jew of his time. Yet, he gave it all up.

Paul counted all of those things loss for something much better. All of the Jewish accomplishments were considered worthless rubbish (dung) since he had become knowledgeable of Jesus Christ. None of those religious achievements could compare to this new relationship with Jesus Christ. The achievements were considered "rubbish" or dung in comparison to having received Jesus Christ as his Lord and Savior. The old way was considered *trash* compared to the *treasure* of the knowledge of Jesus Christ. He lost the *junk* in order to obtain the *Jewel*. Paul was willing to give it all up to know Jesus. He gave up his home in Tarsus. He gave up a comfortable lifestyle in order to travel on three missionary journeys. By giving it all up, he became an outcast among those with strong Jewish ties. When Stephen was stoned by men with the same perspective as Saul, the Scripture said that Saul watched the coats of the stone-throwers (Acts 7:58). After Saul gave up his Jewish pursuit, those same stone-throwers wanted to destroy him (Acts 9:29). Yes, Paul gave up a lot. Was Paul unhappy about it? No, he had all that he needed in Jesus Christ.

The Absence of Righteousness through Ceremonies (9a)

Paul says, "And be found in him, not having mine own righteousness, which is of the law . . ." (3:9a). All of those religious acts were not sufficient. Among his peers, he was considered a top-notch Jew. He probably could have challenged any of his Jewish counterparts and his record would have been more impressive. He probably went beyond the call of duty when it came to keeping the Sabbath, giving the tithe, and fasting. However, his religious record would not stand before the Lord. It was not good enough to make him righteous before the Lord. Every ritual and ceremony could not cause him to be righteous enough. In Galatians 3:10–11, he wrote, "For as many as are of the works of the law are under the curse: for it is written, Cursed is every one that continueth not in all things which are written in the book of the law to do them. But that no man is justified by the law in the sight of God. . . ."

It really did not matter how good Paul's record was under the law. Even if he had a perfect record—and he did not—he still could not be justified in God's sight. Those who operated under the law remained under the curse even when they followed the commandments. When Jesus dealt with the young rich ruler in the Gospel of Mark, it is evident that people did not understand that all of the law had to be followed in order to be saved. The young rich ruler thought he had kept the law from his youth but failed to recognize that he was breaking the first commandment by prioritizing his possessions over God (Mark 10:17–30). In Galatians 5:9, Paul said, "A little leaven leaveneth the whole lump." If you blow it on one of the commandments, you have blown it on all of them.

The Redeemed Relationship (3:9b–10a)

The Correct Approach (9b)

The only way to have true righteousness is through Christ. Paul continued by saying, ". . . But that which is through the faith of Christ . . ." (3:9b). Jesus is the only way back to the Father. Since everyone operating under the law remained under the curse, it was necessary to get rid of the curse before being reconciled to God. The law could not erase the stain of sin from the human race. Jesus Christ took care of the curse that stemmed from Adam. In Romans 5:19, Paul wrote, "For as by one man's disobedience many were made sinners, so by the obedience of one shall many be made righteous." No act of man can create a path to the throne. No ritualistic law or ceremonial law could redeem humanity. Paul said, "For what the law could not do, in that it was weak through the flesh, God sending his own Son in the likeness of sinful flesh, and for sin, condemned sin in the flesh" (Rom. 8:3).

Paul didn't mind the loss because all of his righteous acts combined could not deliver him from sin. Regardless of how many times he kept the Sabbath, he was still a hell-bound sinner. No matter how many times he gave his tithes, he was still a hell-bound sinner. The submission to the law could not wash away his sins. Man was destined for eternal damnation, "but God commendeth his love toward us, in that, while we were yet sinners, Christ died for us" (Rom. 5:8). Faith in Christ was able to accomplish what the law could not.

The Christian's Attire (9c)

When we accept Jesus Christ as Lord and Savior, we receive ". . . the righteousness which is of God by faith" (3:9c). After receiving Christ, we become covered with His righteousness. This imputed righteousness causes us to be justified in spite of our histories being tainted with sin. We have on the new garments of righteousness because of the obedience of God's Son. When God looks at us, He sees saints and not sinners. He sees the blood of His Son covering us from our sins. Satan will try to convince us that our past behavior will prevent us from becoming righteous before God. In a real sense, it is our past behavior that qualifies us. Jesus came and died for all sinners. The Bible says, "For all have sinned, and come short of the glory of God; being justified freely by his grace through the redemption that is in Christ Jesus" (Rom. 3:23–24).

The clothes of righteousness will not keep us from sinning. When some believers try to justify their sins, we often hear them referring to themselves as "sinners saved by grace." The truth to the matter is that if you are saved, you are now a saint engaging in sin. In most of Paul's letters, we read about some sinful problems existing in the churches. However, in most of the letters, we hear Paul refer to the members of those churches as "saints" and not as "sinners saved by grace." (See Romans 1:7; 1 Corinthians 1:2; 2 Corinthians 1:1; Ephesians 1:1; Philippians 1:1; Colossians 1:2.) Paul knew about the fussing and fighting in the Corinthian church, but they were still saints. He knew about the idolatrous worship of some of the Ephesians, but he still called them saints. The reason they were referred to as "saints" instead of "sinners saved by grace" was because their sinful behavior could not cause the covering of the blood to depart from them.

I also believe there is a psychological element connected to Paul's calling them saints. When they heard this title, it served as a reminder of their calling. As a matter fact, in 1 Corinthians 1:2, Paul says, "Unto the church of God which is at Corinth, to them that are sanctified in Christ Jesus, called to be saints. . . ." This calling to be saints involves progressing to that state. In other words, not only were they saints, they were to do all that they could to live up to the title. Yes, we have been covered with righteousness and God desires for the conduct to match the covering.

The Consuming Ambition (10a)

Paul says, ". . . That I may know him . . ." (3:10a). The consuming ambition of Paul was to know more about Jesus. His goal was to learn more about the One responsible for placing him on the right track. With the same energy and vigor that had existed in his pursuit of religious accomplishments earlier, he had set out to learn more about Christ. Paul is speaking of an intimate knowledge. For years he had done all that he could to fight against Him. Now, he was going to try to learn all that he could about Him.

You may ask, "How does a believer get to know Him more?" John says, "And hereby we do know that we know him, if we keep his commandments. He that saith, I know him, and keepeth not his commandments, is a liar, and the truth is not in him" (1 John 2:3–4). We all can get to know Him more by applying the Word of God to our lives. The more we study the Word and become doers of the Word, we will know more and more about Him. In Ephesians 1:17, where Paul prays for the Ephesians, he prayed, "That the God of our Lord Jesus Christ, the Father of glory, may give unto you the spirit of wisdom and revelation in the knowledge of him."

When you learn more about Him, you learn how to trust Him more. This explains Paul's bravery and courage while in prison. His relationship with Jesus Christ gave him all the confidence that he needed to deal with his plight in Rome. When you know Him, you can't doubt Him. If faith is believing and trusting in Him, the more knowledge you have, the more faith you will have in Him. If you are just acquainted with the Lord, it is probably difficult for you to trust in Him when the storms of life are raging. If you know Him, you can have satisfaction in whatever state you are in because you know that He is there with you.

I love the story told about the testimonial service in a local church one Sunday evening. A young man who had recently graduated from college stood and read the twenty-third Psalm. As he read the verses in the passage, his enunciation and pronunciation of each word were perfect. After he finished, the members of the congregation gave him a standing ovation. Later in the service, a senior citizen, using her walking cane, walked down the aisle to the front of the church. She started reciting the twenty-third Psalm. Her enunciation and pronunciation of the words were not perfect.

However, as she recited the passage, tears started flowing from the eyes of the members. Before she finished, some of the members were up on their feet praising God. After the service was over, the young college grad approached the older lady and said, "When I recited the twenty-third Psalm, the people stood and clapped. When you recited the passage, they cried and shouted. Why were the responses different?" The senior citizen looked at him and said, "You know the twenty-third Psalm, but I know the Shepherd."

The Rejected Redeemer (3:10b–11)

The Power of His Resurrection (10b)

Paul not only wanted to know Him, he also wanted to know "the power of his resurrection" (3:10b). Paul realized that victorious living over sin and the flesh required that he continue seeking to know Him, as well as the power of His resurrection. One day, I had a stain in one of my favorite shirts. Someone assured me that a certain cleaning agent would remove this stain from the shirt. I placed it in the washer and poured a capful of the cleaning agent into the washer. After removing my shirt from the washer, I noticed that the evidence of the stain was still there. I concluded that the cleaning agent was not as good as the person had said it was. Later, I read the label on the bottle that contained the cleaning agent. It said, "For tough stains, apply full strength directly on the stain." I placed some of the cleaning agent directly on the stain, and to my amazement the stain was removed. I learned that the ability of the product was based on how the product was used. When the stains are tough, you can't dilute the product.

Although we have been covered by the blood of Jesus, we still have within us the desire to walk according to the flesh. God desires for the believer to be saved, secured, strengthened, and sanctified. This comes when we know the power of His resurrection. When Paul speaks of the power of His resurrection, he is dealing with the things accomplished for us by the resurrection of our Lord and Savior Jesus Christ that lead to victorious living. When Jesus Christ was placed in the borrowed tomb of Joseph of Arimathea, it was a temporary event. On the third day, Jesus was resurrected with all power in His hands. This resurrection power is available to every believer for the purpose of winning the battle over the sinful

Merited Favor: When the Gains Outweigh the Losses 101

nature. A clearer picture of what Paul is dealing with can be seen in Romans 6:3–6.

According to Romans 6, there are several things that happened for us as a result of the power of His resurrection. First, we were *baptized by His grace*. In Romans 6:3, Paul says, "Know ye not, that so many of us as were baptized into Jesus Christ were baptized into his death?" Here, Paul is informing us of what the baptism symbolizes for the believer. When we were baptized, we were baptized into the body of grace. As a result of confessing with our mouths and believing in our hearts, we were baptized into the family of God.

Not only were we baptized by His grace, we were *buried by His grace*. In Romans 6:4, Paul says, "Therefore we are buried with him by baptism into death. . . ." We were buried in baptism as a symbol of the old nature having been crucified and put to death. Thus in Galatians 2: 20, Paul says, "I am crucified with Christ. . . ." And in Romans 6:6, he says, "Knowing this, that our old man is crucified. . . ." The "old man," operating according to orders given by the evil one, had to be crucified and buried. We were all children of wrath, and this nature had to be put to death.

Also, we were *brought up by His grace*. In Romans 6:4b, Paul says, ". . . as Christ was raised up from the dead by the glory of the Father. . . ." We were buried by grace and then brought up by grace. The songwriter put it like this:

> *I was sinking deep in sin, far from the peaceful shore,*
> *Very deeply stained within, sinking to rise no more.*
> *But the Master of the sea heard my despairing cry—*
> *From the waters lifted me; now safe am I.*

It was the love of God that lifted us and raised us up. In Romans 6:5, Paul says, "For if we have been planted together in the likeness of his death, we shall also be in the likeness of his resurrection." This is what Paul means by wanting to "know him, and the power of his resurrection."

Lastly, as a result of knowing the power of His resurrection, we were *branded by His grace*. Since we have been brought up by His grace, Paul says, ". . . even so we also should walk in newness of life" (Rom. 6:4c). The knowledge of the power of His resurrection is seen in how we look now. We have become new creations in

Christ Jesus. The old things have been buried and we should be able to behold a new life.

The Pain of His Rejection (10c)

Next, Paul deals with the knowledge of the suffering of the Savior. As believers, we must come into the knowledge of "the fellowship of His sufferings" (3:10c). Jesus had to suffer for our sakes, and now we must learn how to suffer for His sake. Isaiah 53:3 says, "He is despised and rejected of men; a man of sorrows, and acquainted with grief. . . ." As a believer, Paul could always look at the rejection of Christ as his model. In 2 Corinthians 11:23–28, Paul lists the things he suffered for the cause of Christ. Yet, he kept the faith through all of it. When Paul was tossed out of cities, all he had to do was think about the way Jesus was rejected. When people became angry at what he said in his sermons, all he had to do was think about how they rejected the sermons of Christ. When he received many lashes for his testimonies, all he needed to do was think about how they beat Jesus before placing that cross on His shoulders.

Just like Paul, we should expect seasons of suffering and periods of persecution. However, there is nothing that we could ever witness that could match the suffering of our Lord and Savior Jesus Christ. When it is all said and done, we should be able to say like Paul, "Therefore I take pleasure in infirmities, in reproaches, in necessities, in persecutions, in distresses for Christ's sake: for when I am weak, then am I strong" (2 Cor. 12:10).

The Passion of His Redemption (10d)

Next, Paul says, ". . . Being made conformable unto his death" (3:10d). Paul wanted to have the same passion for the lost as Christ has for the lost. Jesus was willing to die because of this passion for the lost. Jesus did nothing to deserve a death on a cross. He did it for us. Paul wanted to know this passion. This is why Paul could go on missionary journeys, witness shipwrecks, and be thrown in prison. This is why he wasn't worried about the outcome of his imprisonment. He was willing do whatever was necessary to win the lost. He had a passion for the lost.

When we examine the passion for the lost that Paul, Peter, Stephen and others had, it should cause every believer to re-examine his/her commitment to the cause of Christ. Some people will not witness for fear of getting their feelings hurt. Some believers will not witness in fear of some backlash. When we think about someone like Stephen being stoned to death because of his passion for the lost, it should cause us to repent for our lack of evangelistic fervor.

The Promise of His Reward (11)

Paul knew that all of this would lead to a general resurrection of all of those who had received Jesus Christ. In Philippians 3:11, Paul says, "If by any means I might attain unto the resurrection of the dead." In this verse, Paul was not simply dealing with the resurrection of the dead. He knew that this was going to take place. All dead, righteous and unrighteous, will be resurrected. Paul used the Greek term *exanastasis*, which means "out-resurrection." In other words, Paul was confident that his reward for the services he had provided would come in the future. By living a life in the knowledge of Christ and experiencing His suffering, as well as His passion for the lost, Paul knew there was a special reward in store for him and others like him.

All of us are trying to get to heaven. The truth of the matter is that if you are saved, you are bound for heaven. As a matter of fact, you did not do anything to earn that privilege because Jesus paid it all. On the other hand, the "out-resurrection" that Paul speaks of in Philippians 3:11 represents something earned by the believer. Paul is dealing with an achievement acquired by commitment and effort.

When you look at the program from my high school graduation, you will notice an interesting order of the names. There are four names listed, and then the remaining names are in alphabetical order. This represented the order that were to march in and receive our diplomas. The four names listed before the alphabetized names are there for a very special reason. In my high school graduating class, there was a three-way tie for the highest grade point average. Therefore, there were three valedictorians at my graduation. There were over 150 graduates. All of us graduated, but only three were honored as valedictorians of the class and the fourth was honored as the salutatorian. All of us will graduate when the rapture of the church occurs, but some are going to be valedictorians.

Chapter 8

Those Were Not the Good Old Days

Philippians 3:12–14

The Present Responsibilities
    The Personal Status
    The Path Selected
    The Pursued Savior
The Past Regrets
    The Legends of the Past
    The Liabilities of the Past
    The Lessons from the Past
The Promised Reward
    The Forward Progression
    The Focal Point
    The Fabulous Prize

The Present Responsibilities (3:12)

The Personal Status (12a)

In Philippians 3:12a, Paul says, "Not as though I had already attained, either were already perfect. . . ." Paul admits his status in the first part of verse 12. He used the Greek term *teleioo*, which means "perfected or consummated." He knew that he had not arrived. He had not perfected his passions for ministry. He wanted to make this point clear to the reader. He didn't want his friends in Philippi to get the wrong message from this letter. He wasn't trying to paint a picture that he was a better person than anyone else.

Paul had accomplished a lot for the cause of Christ, yet he admitted that he had not arrived. There was still some room for spiritual goals that he needed to reach in his lifetime. He was striving for the day when he could say, "For I am now ready to be offered, and the time of my departure is at hand. I have fought a good fight, I have finished my course, I have kept the faith" (2 Tim. 4:6–7). In other words, Paul knew that his goal of perfection was a lifelong pursuit. Paul knew that perfection would not come until the "Perfect One" came to receive him from this world. This is the only way anyone can reach this state of perfection. However, Paul knew that his life needed to reveal that he was moving in that direction although he had not yet arrived.

There are so many men and women in the Lord that I admire for their spiritual walk. However, I am not naïve. I know they have not attained perfection. They are still striving for perfection in the faith. None of us are perfect, but there should be some evidence of our moving in that direction.

The Path Selected (12b)

Although his personal status had some imperfections, he chose the perfect path. He says, ". . . but I follow after . . ." (3:12b). He was following after righteousness. He was fleeing unrighteousness to follow after righteousness. He knew he could not attain righteousness if he was on the wrong path. Paul had once been on the wrong path. On that path, he had a passion to stamp out Christianity. Now, he is on a different road. He is traveling down *Righteous Road, Heaven's Highway, Blessed Boulevard,* and *Straight Street.* He would have loved to have been stuck in some traffic jams as he traveled—traffic jams caused by so many folks on the road with him! Matthew 7:14 says, "Because strait is the gate, and narrow is the way, which leadeth unto life, and few there be that find it."

The songwriter puts it this way:

> *There's a highway to Heaven.*
> *None can walk up there but the pure in heart.*
> *There's a highway to heaven,*
> *And I'm walking up the King's highway.*

The path that we select has already been paved and prepared. God has drafted the map for us. Psalm 23:3 says, ". . . He leadeth me in the paths of righteousness for his name's sake." Let His Word drive you on the freeway of faith.

The Pursued Savior (3:12c)
Paul says, ". . . If that I may apprehend that for which also I am apprehended of Christ Jesus" (3:12c). The word "apprehend" means "to lay hold of." He wanted to lay hold of the One who had laid hold of him. John 15:16 says, "Ye have not chosen me, but I have chosen you, and ordained you. . . ." Paul was on a mission to get hold of Christ. Yes, he knew that Christ was with him and in him. Yet, there was a desire to see Him. He wasn't going to be satisfied until he was able to lay hold of the One who represented perfection. He wanted to see Jesus face to face. As he traveled down the path of righteousness, he could see his Savior's face more and more clearly.

When we give our lives to Christ, there should be some changes in what we pursue. Instead of pursuing stuff, we should pursue Christ. Our earthly pursuit should be an attempt to be more like Jesus. The more we adapt to the ways of Christ, the more of Christ others are able to see. After being transformed into His image, the day will come when we will be able to see Him face to face. The songwriter said,

Oh, I want to see Him, and look upon His face.
There to see forever of His amazing grace.
On the streets of glory, let me lift my voice.
Cares have passed; I'll be home at last, ever to rejoice.

The Past Regrets (3:13)

The Legends of the Past (13a)
Once again, Paul reiterates his status. In Philippians 3:13a, he says, "Brethren, I count not myself to have apprehended: but this one thing I do, forgetting those things which are behind. . . ." Paul had accomplished so much in his Christian life at the time of this writing. A countless number of people had given their lives to Christ because of his testimony. Churches had been planted and were growing by leaps and bounds because of his missionary journeys. He had inspired so many by his teaching and preaching. There were many healed of their diseases and liberated from their bondage because of his ministry. His spiritual résumé was most impressive. However,

Paul said in Philippians 3:12, "Brethren, I count not myself to have apprehended...."

No matter how much we have done for the cause of Christ, we should never think that we have done enough. We may have been responsible for leading many to Christ, yet there are still some more unsaved people we need to reach. We may have fed many that were hungry, but there are still many more hungry people in this world. We may have encouraged many people who were depressed, distressed and downtrodden, but many more are still hoping to receive words of encouragement. Many of us treat the work of ministry like we do our jobs and after a certain point, we look forward to retirement. In Christ, there is no retirement program as long as we live down here.

Paul knew that he had to forget about the past accomplishments. As impressive as his résumé may have been, Paul knew that the things listed represented past accomplishments. He knew that he had to forget about those accomplishments and keep trying to do more for the cause of Christ. Paul's concentration was on the present and future rather than on the past.

In regard to our spiritual accomplishments in life, we should never think that we have been so successful that we can live off of the successes of the past. OK, you have done some great things. Bravo! But Jesus asks, "What have you done for Me lately?" Forget about the church you built yesterday, and focus on establishing more churches to house the family of God. Forget about your involvement with the outreach and visitation ministry when you were younger and plan on reaching out and visiting others today and in the future.

The Liabilities of the Past (13b)

For many, there are a lot of liabilities or drawbacks of the past that keep them from moving in the right direction. By remembering those things that were behind, Paul's ministry could have become stifled and stagnant. For instance, he could have reflected on those days when he hurt the church by seeking to stamp it out. He could have reflected on the day when he smiled as Stephen was being stoned to death. Those things in his past could have caused Paul to spend most of his time having a pity party rather than leading people to Christ. Instead of focusing on those things in his past, Paul said he was "forgetting those things which are behind" (3:13b). He accepted the forgiveness of the Father through His Son and forgot about those things.

There are people who have allowed the *failures* of the past to hold them back. Before you came to Christ, you may have done some horrible things. After Christ saved you, you had problems letting go of the guilt associated with your actions. Every time you want to commit to ministry, Satan causes that guilt to surface. Satan does not desire for you to recognize the freedom that you have in Christ. You have been liberated from all of those past sins. In Hebrews 10:17, the writer says, "And their sins and iniquities will I remember no more." Since God has forgotten about those past acts of unrighteousness, why can't you?

Some have allowed the *foes* of the past to hold them back. Paul was not accepted by all of the people he came in contact with. As a matter of fact, some people did some horrible and evil things to this soldier of the cross. Paul could have allowed bitterness to keep him from the work of ministry. Had he harbored bitterness for the enemy in his heart, he would have gone on only one missionary journey instead of three. There may have been people in your past that have done some evil things to you. You need to forgive those people so that you can concentrate on the work of ministry. Satan would like for you to spend time trying to figure out how to get even with someone who wounded you in the past instead of focusing on ministry. We are to forgive people. It is not a request; it is a requirement. Matthew 6:15 says, "But if ye forgive not men their trespasses, neither will your Father forgive your trespasses."

Lastly, some people have allowed the *fears* of the past to hold them back from the work of ministry. In the past, we may have had a lot of phobias that would have made the work of ministry difficult. Those fears could be things like the fear of speaking in public or even the fear of being in public. God never calls us out of the darkness into the marvelous light to keep us entangled with the fears of the past. In 2 Timothy 1:7, Paul says, "For God hath not given us the spirit of fear; but of power, and of love, and of a sound mind." Many saints have not discovered the removal of fears because they are still holding on to the thoughts of the way it used to be.

The Lessons from the Past (13c)

When Paul speaks of forgetting in the text, it is selective forgetting. We should never forget about everything in our past. For instance, we should forget about those sins of the past, but we must never forget the Lord saving us from those sins. We should remember all of those valuable lessons we learned from the past. We should remember certain things from the past because some of those past events will help us in the present and future. Many of those memories can launch us into "reaching forth unto those things which are before" (3:13c).

Your present testimony points to the past as well as to the future. From the past, your testimony simply means that you made it through the test and trials. In the future, you are going to be tested. The present testimony connected to the past will help you keep the faith when the future test or trial comes.

The general rule of ministry should be: "I will forget everything that prevents ministry, and I will remember everything that promotes ministry." Throughout the Old Testament, God continually reminded Israel about their deliverance from Egyptian bondage. He reminded them of how their needs were met in the wilderness. He continued to remind them of how He gave them the land flowing with milk and honey. Why did He continue to remind them? It was because He wanted them to remember it. The lessons from the past would help them in the future.

The Promised Reward (3:14)

The Forward Progression (14a)

Philippians 3:14a says, "I press toward the mark...." Paul used an athletic term to describe his pursuit. He is talking about pressing on even when the pressure is on. He is speaking of pressing forward even when there is a strain on your spiritual muscles. When cramps come, keep pressing. When fatigue comes, keep pressing forward. When you reach a hurdle, jump it and keep pressing on. Paul was determined that he was not going to turn around because he remembered the words of Jesus when he said, "No man, having put his hand to the plough, and looking back, is fit for the kingdom of God" (Luke 9:62).

As we press on, there are some pointers that can reduce the strain. Hebrews 12:1b says, "... Let us lay aside every weight, and the sin which doth so easily beset us, and let us run with patience the race that is set before us." There are times when we allow sin to weigh us down. When we continue to engage in sin and try to run this race, it creates strain. Another helpful pointer is to work out before engaging in the exercise. As you prepare to press on in the race, you need to do some warm-up exercises. How do you warm up for this spiritual race? You do it by having a serious personal Bible study program as well as a strong prayer life. In 2 Timothy 2:15, Paul says, "Study to show thyself approved unto God, a workman that needeth not to be ashamed, rightly dividing the word of truth." Studying the Word will help reduce the strain. In Ephesians 6, where Paul talked about the need to wear the whole armor of God when we are in the Christian race, he ended by saying, "Praying always with all prayer and supplication . . ." (Eph. 6:18).

The Focal Point (14b)

Notice the focal point for Paul. He says, "I press toward the mark for the prize of the high calling of God in Christ Jesus" (3:14). You must stay focused in order to run this race. Hebrews 12:2 says, "Looking unto Jesus the author and finisher of our faith; who for the joy that was set before him endured the cross, despising the shame, and is set down at the right hand of the throne of God." Sometimes we get so caught up in who else is running on the track that we lose focus. Instead of looking at the other lanes, keep your eyes on the Author and Finisher of our faith.

One day, I asked a member of the church where I pastor why he behaved a certain way when I saw him driving. I said, "Morris, why don't you stop ignoring me and wave back at me when I wave at you on the road?"

He looked at me and said, "Pastor, I wasn't ignoring you. I just keep my eyes on the road so that I won't have an accident." As believers, we need to keep our eyes on Christ so that we will not have an accident. Satan desires to distract us and keep us from traveling to our destination. If you don't want to have a wreck, keep your eyes on the mark.

When we focus on the mark, God will reveal some of the tricks of the enemy in advance. In traffic we have to keep our focus on what is happening around us in order to see other drivers running lights or coming out of side streets unexpectedly. There are times we have to slow down to avoid accidents. In the same way, as we focus our attention on the Author and Finisher of our faith, He will show us Satan's ambushes up ahead and slow us down in other areas to avoid spiritual wrecks in our lives. The Author and Finisher of our faith prepares us for Satan's sneaky attacks, but we have to rivet our attention on Him.

My middle son has tried repeatedly to scare me as I step out of my office at home. He hides behind the bedroom door, and as I turn the corner he jumps up and yells. He hasn't been able to scare me yet. The reason he can't scare me is because as I turn the corner to go into the bedroom, there is a long mirror on the dresser. I can see him before I get to the area where he is hiding. When we keep our eyes on Christ, He reveals the schemes of the enemy in advance.

The Fabulous Prize (14c)

One day, the race will be over and Paul's desire was to receive "the prize of the high calling of God in Christ Jesus" (14c). When you have almost made it to the finish line, you can say with Paul, ". . . I have finished my course. . . . Henceforth there is laid up for me a crown of righteousness, which the Lord, the righteous judge, shall give me at that day: and not to me only, but unto all them also that love his appearing" (2 Tim. 4:7–8). Jesus is at the award ceremony and will crown those in the race. Crowns are not given based on skill, style or speed. As long as you finish, you will be crowned.

Although every believer will be crowned, some believers will receive some extra stars in their crowns. For instance, during the Millennium, some believers will be able to rule one thousand years with Jesus Christ. This will be an extra star for some believers.

But Paul's focus was not on an earthly prize. His prize was greater than anything the world could offer him for he had a special account in heaven. When we keep our eyes focused on Christ, we will eventually receive our treasure chest. This treasure chest is better than a pot of gold at the end of the rainbow. In fact, the gold will be so plentiful that we will be able to walk on it. The pearls are so plentiful that we will be able to enter through twelve high gates made of pearl. The walls will be made of diamonds and other special jewels. Mansions will be available for all. In Matthew 6:20–21, Jesus said, "But lay up for yourselves treasures in heaven, where neither moth nor rust doth corrupt, and where thieves do not break through nor steal: For where your treasure is, there will your heart be also."

CHAPTER 9

The Wheat and the Tares

Philippians 3:15–21

The Walk of the Family
 The Mature Parishioners
 The Misguided Participants
 The Main Point
The Wolves in the Field
 The Preacher on the Frontline
 The Practitioners of the Faith
 The Pretenders in the Fight
 The Perdition of the Future
The World of the Faithful
 The Citizenship of the Saints
 The Coming of the Savior
 The Changing of the Servants
 The Creator of the Substance

The Walk of the Family (3:15–16)

The Mature Parishioners (15a)

In Philippians 3:15a, Paul said, "Let us therefore, as many as be perfect, be thus minded. . . ." If you are not careful, this verse can appear to conflict with another verse. In Philippians 3:12, Paul admitted that he was not perfect, but here, just three verses later, he says he is perfect. There is an explanation for this play on words. In verse 12, the word translated perfect is the Greek verb *teleioo*, in the perfect tense. In the perfect tense, the word means "completed or perfected." But here, Paul used the word *telios,* which means "to progress or mature to a certain stage." Paul knew he had not arrived or perfected anything, but he knew he was a mature Christian. The maturity of a believer is seen in his character, conversation, and conduct. Paul was walking in the Spirit and not in the flesh. In 1 Corinthians 2:6–3:3, Paul deals with the three states of existence in the life of humanity. There is the natural man who does not know Jesus Christ. There is the carnal man who has received Jesus Christ as Savior but not as Lord. Lastly, there is the spiritual man who can interpret the things of God because the Spirit of God is in control of his life.

Paul was not the only spiritually mature believer. There were those among the Philippians who were "thus minded," or likeminded. There were others who had reached this stage of development in their Christian walk. There were others in the family of faith allowing the Holy Spirit to control their lives. It was evident by their lifestyles. They were applying the Word of God to their lives. Although they had not arrived, they were walking in the right direction. In 1 John 2:12–14, John used a system like Paul to identify the spiritual stages of believers. He talks about little children, children, young men, and fathers. John's use of these terms suggests that there are stages of development in the Christian's life. As a new convert, you are a child and you start maturing to adulthood. The maturity of the believer is not based on the number of years a person has been saved. The maturity of a believer is evidenced by a person's move from salvation to sanctification.

The Misguided Participants (15b)

Not everyone in the church at Philippi considered Paul a spiritual hero. As a matter of fact, Paul addressed some of them in Philippians 3:2–3. These members represented the "otherwise minded" in the group. Satan is going to make sure that there are always some people with an anti-leader spirit in the church. I am not speaking of someone who disagrees periodically with those in leadership. I am dealing with those who always disagree with those in leadership. They are known for always saying the negative things and never any positive things. They are always criticizing and never complimenting.

It could be that some of those otherwise minded thought they had arrived. When Paul announced that he had not arrived in verse 12, these members probably nodded their heads in agreement. They were probably the ones who voted against sending a love offering to Paul while he was on his missionary journeys and while he was in prison. Whatever the case, Paul knew there were some that were otherwise minded. Some of the people who received this title may have listened to some of those Judaizers and felt that pressing toward the mark involved maintaining rituals, ceremonies, and traditions.

Since Paul was knowledgeable of their existence, he ministered to them like he ministered to everyone else in the family. By the way, it is a sign of spiritual maturity when you can minister to those who don't particularly care for you. Paul did not love them any less than he loved the other Philippians. Paul realized that one of the challenges of ministry was to guide those who were misguided. We should never mistreat the misguided people in our midst. When they frown, we should smile. When they say negative things about us, we should say more positive things about them.

I love comparing biblical characters. I love to compare David with Saul. Because of David's fame after killing Goliath, Saul became insanely jealous of David. David was guided by God while Saul was misguided by evil spirits. On one occasion, Saul went to the witch of Endor to seek advice about God's kingdom. While Saul was being misguided by evil spirits, one of his main goals was to put David to death. There were times while Saul pursued David that God demonstrated how the misguided should be treated by those who are allowing the Holy Spirit to guide them. On several occasions, while Saul sought to kill David, God allowed David to sneak up on Saul. But instead of killing Saul, David always spared his life. If David had killed Saul instead of sparing his life, David would have become just as misguided as Saul.

The Main Point (16)

Paul says, "Nevertheless, whereto we have already attained, let us walk by the same rule, let us mind the same thing" (3:16). Paul was determined not to spend his time in this letter debating over issues. The enemy loves for us to spend all of our time debating over who's right and who's wrong in the family when there are so many spiritual things to be done. One day, Martha tried to cause Jesus to enter into one of these debates. Jesus had stopped by the home of Mary and Martha. Martha was in the kitchen preparing things since her friend Jesus had come by. On the other hand, Mary just sat at the feet of Jesus to listen to every word that came from His mouth. Martha became frustrated and complained to Jesus because she was doing all of the work while Mary sat there and did nothing. Jesus answered her, ". . . Martha, Martha, thou art careful and troubled about many things: but one thing is needful: and Mary hath chosen that good part, which shall not be taken away from her" (Luke 10:41–42). Jesus did not take the time to debate the issue. He simply revealed what was best.

In Philippians 3:16, Paul used military terminology when he wrote, ". . . let us walk by the same rule, let us mind the same thing." As soldiers in the army of the Lord, he didn't want them focusing on the other soldiers' jobs. He wanted them to stay focused on the battle. Paul wanted them to stay in line. He knew that a believer cannot be successful in the fight if he or she is not attentive, alert, and of one accord. Satan loves for believers to fight and fuss among themselves instead of staying in line. Satan knows that the more we fuss, the less we witness.

In essence, Paul said, "Stay in line by following the military manual, the Word of God." In verse 15, Paul had said, ". . . God shall reveal even this unto you." If we stay in line by walking by the same rule, God will reveal everything that we need to know. With the Word of God as our guidebook, even the misguided can be brought back into line.

When I was a kid, I was invited to attend a dance. The problem was that I couldn't dance. I had two left feet. I decided that I would not attend the dance. My big brother wanted to know why I wasn't going and I told him and showed him that I couldn't dance. My clapping and steps were so off-beat that you would have thought I was tone deaf. My brother turned the music on and did something interesting. He picked me up and placed my feet on his feet and I learned how to coordinate my steps. He took my hands and caused me to clap on beat. I was the best ten-year-old dancer at the dance. Paul was saying, "Let's place our feet on the feet of Jesus so we can stay in line."

The Wolves in the Field (3:17–19)

The Preacher on the Frontline (17a)

Philippians 3:17 says, "Brethren, be followers together of me...." At the end of this verse, Paul used the word example. The Greek word for example is *tupos*, which means "pattern." It is like making an imprint of a figure and tracing it from the imprint. Paul wanted them to use him as a pattern for living. He was not saying, "Do as I say and not as I do." Instead, Paul was living by the sermons he preached. He wanted the saints of God to use him as a pattern. It is good when a preacher can say what Paul said in this verse. Paul gave them permission to look at him and follow him as he followed Christ. His pattern was patterned after Christ.

Peter also talked about the walk of the preacher. He wrote, "Feed the flock of God which is among you, taking the oversight thereof, not by constraint, but willingly; not for filthy lucre, but of a ready mind; neither as being lords over God's heritage, but being ensamples [examples] to the flock" (1 Pet. 5:2–3). Every preacher of the gospel should preach with both his lips and his life. As a matter of fact, when he preaches with his life, the words from his lips are received better by the hearers. We should be able to have others be able to trace the spiritual imprint of our lives.

The Reverend Jeffrey Johnson of Indianapolis tells a wonderful story to support this point. One day, he went outside to shovel snow from his driveway. His son wanted to go with him, but the snow was too deep for him. His son figured out a way to get to his father. He put on his snowshoes and found the imprints of his father's footsteps to walk out to him. His son was using his father's footsteps as a guide to find his way. We should remember that there are others using the imprint of our footsteps as a pattern. We must be careful where and how we walk.

The Practitioners of the Faith (17b)

There were others practicing what they preached. Paul suggested: "... and mark them which walk so as ye have us for an ensample" (3:17b). Believers could pattern their lives not only after Paul's life, but also after other saints who were living holy lives. Hopefully, in a church there are several spiritual people to imitate. They were not able to see Paul on a regular basis because his traveling and imprisonment prevented it. However, there were others in their midst they could imitate. There were people like Silas, Lydia, Epaphroditus, Timothy and others who were committed to Christ. How can you determine who to follow and who not to follow? The psalmist gave us a beautiful description of the godly man: "Blessed is the man that walketh not in the counsel of the ungodly, nor standeth in the way of sinners, nor sitteth in the seat of the scornful. But his delight is in the law of the LORD; in his law doth he meditate day and night" (Psa. 1:1–2). There are certain places spiritual people will not go. There are certain things spiritual people will not do. There are certain people spiritual people will not fellowship with. They will live according to the book that they meditate on day and night. Don't be fooled by their ability to recite Scripture. It is the reciting of the Word accompanied by the rehearsing of the Word that authenticates a disciple. You can tell who to follow by where they walk, stand, and sit.

The Pretenders in the Fight (18)

Paul says, "For many walk, of whom I have told you often, and now tell you even weeping, that they are the enemies of the cross of Christ" (3:18). Paul wanted the Philippians to know that there were some pretenders around. First, he dealt with the *walk of the pretenders*. In using the term "walk," Paul implied that there were some walking in their midst who were not genuine. We should never think that every name written on the church roll is recorded in the Lamb's book of life. There are those in the midst who have not given their lives to Jesus Christ, although they may be faithful in their attendance and active in various ministries.

Then we have the *warning about the pretenders*. This is not the first time Paul has told the Philippians about the pretenders. As Paul traveled from city to city, there were pretenders following him to try and uproot what he had planted. As Paul sought to establish churches, these pretenders tried to destroy them. Satan will always try to destroy things established by God. Satan knows he can't destroy the institutions of God, but he will do all that he can to stir up trouble. Paul wanted to remind the saints again and again about the pretenders. Paul was like a boxer's trainer. When a boxer is in the ring, the trainer does not sit back during the boxing match and say, "I have done my job training him." No, the trainer is in the boxer's corner reminding him to watch out for the opposition's left hook. Paul wanted to warn them as often as possible because he did not want the saints to let down their guards. If they became spiritually relaxed, Paul knew the pretenders would throw an uppercut and knock them out.

Next, the text deals with Paul's *weeping for the pretenders*. Paul was weeping as he wrote this portion of the letter. As mentioned repeatedly in this book, Paul spent most of his time rejoicing. But all of a sudden, the mood changes. What could cause Paul's move from shouting to sighing? What would cause his tears to change from tears of joy to tears of sorrow? He is weeping for them because he wanted them to be saved from their sins. He wanted them to taste the goodness of salvation in Christ Jesus. The thought of people being lost should cause believers to weep. Paul did not want to see anyone die in his or her sins and spend eternity in hell. Paul wanted his weeping to change to rejoicing. If the pretenders would stop pretending, he would start rejoicing. Psalm 126:6 says, "He that goeth forth and weepeth, bearing precious seed, shall doubtless come again with rejoicing, bringing his sheaves with him." Paul wanted the Philippians to respond to the urging of the Holy Spirit in their lives.

Lastly, Paul dealt with the *wickedness of the pretenders*. In Philippians 3:18, he refers to them as "enemies of the cross." When Jesus was on the scene, there were a lot of self-righteous people doing so many wicked things to our Lord and Savior. Some of them gathered around the cross and mocked Jesus. They were enemies of the cross. The enemies were still alive and well in Philippi and everywhere else. The most important symbol of the Christian faith was opposed by some of the members of this church. Their opposition to the cross of Calvary caused their church membership to be in vain. If there is no cross, there will not be a crown.

The Perdition of the Future (19)

Paul listed some specific details about the wickedness of the foe. First, he dealt with *the destiny of the wicked*. In Philippians 3:19a, Paul says, "Whose end is destruction. . . ." The word for destruction is "perdition." Perdition is the destruction, ruin, or waste, especially through the eternal destruction brought upon the wicked by God. The New Testament uses the phrase "son of perdition" twice. One is a reference to Judas Iscariot and the other time it is a reference to the Antichrist. In both cases, we see a progression of evil that leads to destruction.

2 Peter 3:7 says, "But the heavens and earth, which are now, by the same word are kept in store, reserved unto fire against the day of judgement and perdition of ungodly men." Psalm 37:12–13 says, The wicked plotteth against the just, and gnasheth upon him with his teeth. The LORD shall laugh at him: for he seeth that his day is coming." This is one of the reasons why believers should not envy the wicked. It may appear as if good things are happening to evil people, but remember, there is a doomsday ahead.

Next, Paul deals with *the desire of the wicked*. The desire of the wicked is sensual. In Philippians 3:19, Paul said, "Whose end is destruction, whose God is their belly. . . ." Their goal was to fill their bellies. When Paul used the term belly, he was dealing not only with their digestive systems, but also with the satisfaction (albeit temporary) of the urges and cravings of life. The lust of the flesh was in total control. There was nothing spiritual about their appetites. They were simply living for the moment. The desire of the wicked involves doing whatever it takes to feel good. They are not concerned about anyone but themselves. It is like a drug addict trying to get drugs in order to deal with the craving. Just like an addict, the wicked person will do whatever it takes to support his/her habit.

Next, Paul says, ". . . whose glory is in their shame, who mind earthly things" (3:19). Here Paul deals with *the delight of the wicked*. They not only enjoyed doing what they were doing; they also had the audacity to justify their behavior. Although it was wrong, they claimed that it was right and were happy about it. Their glory had become their shame according to Paul. They would say, "If doing it is wrong, we don't want to be right." They enjoyed their indulgence and had no desire to discontinue it. As a matter of fact, they thought others were on the wrong path and that they were missing out on the pleasures of life. The wicked will challenge your righteous behavior and try their best to disciple you to their way of living. In Isaiah 5:20–21, we read, "Woe unto them that call evil good, and good evil; that put darkness for light, and light for darkness; that put bitter for sweet, and sweet for bitter! Woe unto them that are wise in their own eyes, and prudent in their own sight!"

He concludes his description by addressing *the devotion of the wicked*. They had their minds set on earthly things. This is what they were devoted to. Since the world was their devotion, they had no desire to discuss the afterlife. The discussion of hell did not cause fear to surface in their hearts. When heaven was mentioned, they viewed their earthly goals as heavenly pursuits. They wanted to get all that they could while they could. They were more concerned about gaining the world than they were about losing their souls.

The World of the Faithful (3:20–21)

The Citizenship of the Saints (20a)

In Philippians 3:20, Paul says, "For our conversation is in heaven. . . ." The word used for conversation is *politeuma*. It refers to the seat of government in which we have citizenship. Paul says that our citizenship or conversation is not of this world. Please note the tense of the verb. He did not say that their citizenship *will be* in heaven, but that it *is* in heaven. This world is not our home. In Ephesians 2:6, Paul says, "And hath raised us up together, and made us sit together in heavenly places in Christ Jesus." Since this world is not our home, we should not act as if we are here to stay. We are presently seated with Christ in heaven.

As citizens of heaven, we are conduct ourselves accordingly. Although we are in a foreign land, we are still required to govern our lives by the rules of heaven. In a real sense, we are citizens of two worlds. One is a temporary citizenship. We have a visa for temporary citizenship here on earth. However, our eternal home is in heaven. One day, the visa will expire on this side. The expiration of the visa will end either by our physical death or the rapture of the church.

The Coming of the Savior (20b)

In Philippians 3:20, Paul continued by saying, ". . . from whence also we look for the Saviour, the Lord Jesus Christ." One day, the King of the country that governs us is coming to take us home. He is home now sitting on the throne. However, one day our Savior is going to come from home to take us back home. Just as John the Baptist served as the forerunner for His first trip to this world, we are now the forerunners preparing for His next trip down here. But

His next trip will be different from the first trip He made to earth. He came in meekness the first time. He will come in His majesty the next time. Although He came as a Lamb the first time, He will come as the Lion of the tribe of Judah next time.

When Paul speaks of Christ's coming in this verse, he is not speaking of the second coming of Christ referred to in Scripture. When we read of the second coming of Christ in Scripture, it is a reference to the time when He comes to judge the world of its sins. The time of which Paul speaks in this text is not the time when He will come all of the way to the earth. The time that Paul is talking about here refers to the time when Jesus will come and we will go to meet Him in the air, referred to as the Rapture. After this, there will be a seven-year period called the Great Tribulation, and at the end of this period will be the Second Coming.

The word translated "look for" in this verse is *apekdechomai*, which means "an anticipated event" or "to eagerly expect." From the moment of Christ's departure in the first chapter of Acts, the church has eagerly awaited His return. The saints from the formative years of the church looked for Jesus to return at any moment. They didn't know when it would happen, but they stayed prepared for it. As believers, we should eagerly anticipate His return. As a matter of fact, we should anticipate it even more than the early church did because everything necessary to be fulfilled before His return has already occurred.

Next to the piano at my home is a backpack that belongs to my four-year-old son. It is always packed. If Charles is going to leave at anytime, he is packed and ready. Jesus can come back at any time now. I am looking forward to His return. He could return while you are reading this book. Are you packed and prepared? Do you have your spiritual backpack ready?

The Changing of the Servants (21a)

In Philippians 3:21, Paul says, "Who shall change our vile body, that it may be fashioned like unto his glorious body...." As ambassadors of Christ on this side, we are weighted down by a burden. In Romans 8:18–19, Paul reminds us, "For I reckon that the sufferings of this present time are not worthy to be compared with the glory which shall be revealed in us. For the earnest expectation of the creature waiteth for the manifestation of the sons of God." When Paul used the term "vile bodies," he was referring to worn-out bodies. Suffering produces wounds. Our bodies are filled with the scars and scrapes of service. However, in 1 Corinthians 15:51–52, Paul says, "Behold, I show you a mystery; We shall not all sleep, but we shall all be changed, in a moment, in the twinkling of an eye, at the last trump. . . ." 1 John 3:2 says, "Beloved, now are we the sons of God, and it doth not yet appear what we shall be: but we know that, when he shall appear, we shall be like him; for we shall see him as he is."

When He comes to take us home, we will receive new bodies. The new bodies have not been given to any of the saints yet. I often hear people referring to loved ones who have died as walking around heaven with painless bodies. This is not the case. It is true that their souls are in heaven. This is what Paul meant when he wrote, "We are confident, I say, and willing rather to be absent from the body, and to be present with the Lord" (2 Cor. 5:8). I have also heard people talk about the decayed bodies of people coming back together when Jesus returns. This can't be accurate because it would mean that old bodies would inherit the kingdom. Instead, one day, the souls of all the saints will be reunited with some transfigured bodies.

The Creator of the Substance (21b)

How can bodies that have been destroyed be refashioned and transfigured? How can the dead be resurrected? How can we receive glorious bodies? Paul says, ". . . Whereby he is able to even to subdue all things unto himself" (3:21b). The word able is the translation of the Greek word *dynamai*. It is a reference to explosive power. The Lord is able to do it. All He has to do is speak it into existence. The One who created us the first time will do it again. It is going to be a different body. It is going to be more like the resurrected body of Jesus Christ.

When the time comes, Jesus will do just as He did at the grave of Lazarus. After Lazarus died, Jesus went to the grave and said, ". . . Lazarus, come forth" (John 11:43). He had to be specific and call him by his name so that everyone in that cemetery would not get up. Death and the grave must release us and let us go. Will Jesus have to call us by our names? No, this will not be necessary. He will probably just say, "Saints, come forth." First, the dead in Christ will go to Him followed by the saints who are alive.

Chapter 10

Dealing with Discord Among Disciples

Philippians 4:1–5

The Beautiful Introduction
    The Proper Approach
    The Preacher's Admiration
    The Pauline Admonition
The Burdensome Issue
    Division in the Church
    Directives to the Clergy
    Discussion of Their Contributions
The Brilliant Instructions
    The Awesome Atmosphere of Praise
    The Adjusted Attitude of People
    The Apparent Appeal to Prepare

The Beautiful Introduction (4:1)

The Proper Approach (1a)

In this verse, it sounds like Paul is using the old cliché that says, "You can catch flies quicker with honey than with vinegar." In this chapter, Paul will address a subject that he has touched on repeatedly in the letter. However, before doing it, he says, "Therefore, my brethren dearly beloved and longed for . . ." (4:1a). One of the difficult chores of ministry involves addressing the sins of saints. As leaders, we must not sit back and ignore the sinful behavior of those who are members of the faith. When we address the believer or believers at fault, we must express love for them. Too often, we *angrily attack* those engaging in sin rather than *affectionately approaching* them. In Galatians 6:1, Paul says, "Brethren, if a man be overtaken in a fault, ye which are spiritual, restore such an one in the spirit of meekness; considering thyself, lest thou also be tempted." The *meek approach* can minister to the person much quicker than the *mean approach*.

Paul reminds the church of his love for them and how much he missed being with them. The expression of love can help to get the pending message across. When a person knows that genuine love exists, he or she can better receive the advice that one is going to give. When a person knows that genuine love exists, the information that follows is viewed as concern rather than criticism. Paul approached this issue properly by expressing his love for the saints.

There are times when the proper approach is perceived as the improper approach at the time of correction. When I was a child, my parents always talked about their love for me just before they tanned my hide. During the time of the correcting, I wanted to know, "What's love got to do with it?" As I matured, I realized that they were trying to prevent me from witnessing some hardships down the road. They had to do it to keep someone else from doing it later.

The Preacher's Admiration (1b)

Paul called the Philippians his "joy and crown" (3:1b). Not only did Paul love them dearly, joy flooded his soul when he thought about them. The Philippians were so special to him. Just the thought of them caused a smile to surface on his face. It is wonderful when the thought of people can cause you to *rejoice* rather than *regret*. While attending seminary in Arizona, I was away from home weeks at a time. Whenever I started getting lonely or overwhelmed, I opened my wallet and pulled out the family picture. Just seeing the picture of my wife and three sons gave me a boost. This is the same way Paul viewed the Philippians. The thought of his friends in Philippi helped him deal with his imprisonment. When the days were rough, he would think about them and get excited.

Not only were they a joy to Paul, he called them his crown as well. There are two words used in Paul's epistles for crowns. One is the crown of a leader, *diadema*, the crown of governmental authority. The other is *stephanos*, the crown of a victor that was awarded in the

Greek games when a person won an athletic event. Paul used the term *stephanos*, when he talked about "the crown of righteousness" in 2 Timothy 4:8. But the crown mentioned in Philippians 4:1 is a *diadema* crown. He is proud to be their leader. As their leader, he is able to write them and give them some spiritual advice. It is like a decree from a king to the subjects that make up the kingdom. Paul is proud to be their leader.

The Pauline Admonition (1c)

In most of Paul's letters, he encouraged the saints to stand or stand fast (1 Cor. 16:13; Gal. 5:1; Eph. 6:11–14; 1 Thess. 3:8; 2 Thess. 2:15). Paul admonished them repeatedly to take a stand for righteousness. In Philippians 4:1, he says, ". . . Stand fast in the Lord, my dearly beloved." He did not want them to lose their footing in the Lord. We lose our footing when we stray from the truth of God's Word. As we try our best to stand fast, Satan tries to do all that he can to cause us to slip.

Following an ice storm in Dallas, some of the kids from the neighborhood were outside trying to have fun. The icy conditions prevented them from having fun because they started slipping down and falling on the hard ice. As the children tried to make it back to their houses from their front yards, they repeatedly slipped and fell. I had taken my middle son outside with me while I carried the trash can to the back yard. He was only four years old and stood still while the other children continued to slip and fall. One of the boys asked him, "Charles, why are you just standing there?"

Charles responded by saying, "I'm going to stand right here until my father comes to help me in." When issues surface and the devil tries to cause you to slip, stand fast until the Father comes to help you.

The Burdensome Issue (4:2–3)

Division in the Church (4:2)

Throughout this letter, Paul has planted seeds of truth in the fertile soil of the Philippian church. Now, he really unloads his wagon. I can imagine that when Epaphroditus arrived, he told the Christians in Philippi to spread the word about a special service being held to read the letter from Paul. As the saints gathered, they waited with tiptoe anticipation to hear what Paul had to say. Can you imagine the assembly sitting and listening to the letter being read? I am sure the reading was periodically interrupted with applause and people saying, "Amen." Throughout the reading, someone probably shouted, "Praise the Lord." When the person reading the letter got to the section where Paul said, "I love you and miss you," someone probably said, "We miss you and love you, too."

All of a sudden, there is a shift in the letter. Philippians 4:2 continues, "I beseech Euodias, and beseech Syntyche, that they be of the same mind in the Lord." He brought the issue out into the open at last. In the first three chapters, he had touched on the issue. Now, he spelled it out. In Philippians 1:10–12, he addressed the issue. In Philippians 2:1–5, he got closer to the issue. In Philippians 3:15–17, he got even closer to the issue. Now, in Philippians 4:2, he lets the hammer down. Division and disharmony had made its way into the church. There were two women in the assembly who did not get along with each other. Paul did not reveal what the squabble was over. It was something probably as insignificant as the color of the drapes or carpet for the church. It could have been something as insignificant as the color of some choir robes or ushers' uniforms. We are not told what the problem was, but the women who caused the problem had their names called. There are times when there is no other way to address a problem than to bring it up before the entire family.

The same church that had been started by women had now been divided by women. There was probably a hush all over the place. I would not be surprised if they didn't make matters worse by pointing the finger. They probably looked at Epaphroditus with anger and said to themselves, "Why did he go up to Rome and tell Paul about us?" That is the reaction that often surfaces when we have been caught. It's not new. In the Garden of Eden, the same thing took place. Instead of admitting their faults, Adam and Eve pointed fingers at someone other than themselves. Instead of saying, "I know he is right and I need to get back on track," some of those at Philippi probably got angry.

Directives to the Clergy (4:3a)

Immediately, Paul told the pastor of the Philippians to get busy ministering to these sisters. Paul knew that the sisters needed some help in dealing with this problem. Therefore, he says, "And I entreat thee also, true yokefellow, help those women" (4:3a). We don't know how long this feud had been going on. It had probably existed for a while since it had been discussed with Paul. It was probably one of the things on his list of things to tell Paul about that Epaphroditus now regretted sharing with Paul. The church members had probably done all they could do about the situation, and revealing it to Paul was a last resort. There were probably some deep scars and wounds that existed between Euodias and Syntyche. Paul knew they needed to have some ongoing spiritual counseling to end the feud.

He tells the pastor or maybe Epaphroditus to do all that they could to help resolve the issue so that they could focus on kingdom building. There are times when I call brothers and sisters in the Lord to the carpet. When they come in complaining about another brother or sister in the Lord, I request that we come together with our Bibles and work through the problem. It takes the Word of God to soothe the sores and mend the broken hearts. Instead of taking the side of one or the other, I try to make sure that I stay on the Lord's side.

Discussion of Their Contributions (4:3b)

Paul softens the blow by reminding the whole congregation of their contributions. He says, ". . . help those women which laboured with me in the gospel, with Clement also, and with others my fellow labourers, whose names are in the book of life" (4:3b). These women not only knew the Lord, they were also women who served the Lord. Paul considered their involvement in ministry as an important piece of the spiritual puzzle. Their gifts and talents had been covered up by this disharmony between them. However, their past involvement in ministry revealed the sincerity of their commitment to Christ. They had labored in the ministry alongside many saints in the past.

Another reason Paul spoke of their salvation and service is to reveal something to the rest of the body of Christ. He didn't want the church to give up on them. There are times when we allow the wrong of a person to erase that which is right. Their names were in the Lamb's book of life and their gifts were valuable to the body of Christ. There may have been some people who said, "They can't really be saved and be acting the way they are acting." Paul wanted to make sure this kind of talk was squashed. We should never give up on God's children. They may have strayed, but they are still precious to the Lord. It is easy to say, "We can get along without them." However, it is better to say, "We need their gifts operating in this church."

The Brilliant Instructions (4:4–5)

The Awesome Atmosphere of Praise (4)

What a wonderful way to refocus. This information about the two women must have caused mouths to fly open. Everyone waited with anticipation to hear the next line of the letter. It was read: "Rejoice in the Lord always: and again I say, Rejoice" (4:4). Paul told them to rejoice in the Lord and repeated it. That's the best way to deal with division. When we stay focused on the Lord, we don't have time for divisions. We will be too busy praising Him. An atmosphere of praise causes the environment of discord to dissipate. An atmosphere of praise creates a scene of harmony.

How can a person rejoice when he or she has been offended by another? How can a person rejoice when the person sitting on the same pew lied on him? How can a person rejoice when his heart has been broken? It is not easy to rejoice, but it is easy to "rejoice in the Lord." When we rejoice in the Lord, it means that we take our attention off ourselves and others, focusing solely on Him. When division surfaces in the family of faith, someone should stand and read Psalm 34:1 or Psalm 103:1–4 out loud.

I have also discovered that it is impossible to bless the Lord at all times and be mad at your brother or sister at the same time. When you start blessing the Lord and remembering all His benefits, including His forgiveness of your iniquities, it helps you to forgive people who have offended you.

The Adjusted Attitude of People (5a)

Paul says, "Let your moderation be known unto all men" (4:5a). The word moderation deals with forbearance and gentleness. Paul was telling those sisters to exercise gentleness. He wanted them to develop a selfless attitude about life. It was a plea to forbear whatever surfaced for the Lord's sake. It is not always a matter about who is right or wrong. Who cares if the best color for the new carpet is red or blue? If my thoughts are different from yours, why should it cause us to fall out with one another?

We should never allow issues to keep us from doing what Paul instructed us to do in Ephesians: "Let all bitterness, and wrath, and anger, and clamour, and evil speaking, be put away from you, with all malice: And be ye kind one to another, tenderhearted, forgiving one another, even as God for Christ's sake hath forgiven you" (Eph. 4:31–32). If we give place to the devil, it will lead to evil things happening. When we live selflessly, we will be quick to reconcile with our brothers and sisters in Christ.

The Apparent Appeal to Prepare (5b)

Philippians 4:5b says, ". . . The Lord is at hand." Paul did not record this to imply that these sisters would miss out on the rapture of the church if the Lord returned while this feud was going on. By having their names written in the Lamb's book of life, they would be included in the Rapture. Every saved person will make it to heaven. Paul wanted them to know that it would be a shame for Jesus to return and catch them acting this way. Jesus should not return and find saints squabbling and disciples divided. He should find us loving one another.

The other reason for reminding them of the Lord's return is connected to ministry. There is too much work for us to do, and we don't have time to sit around mad at each other. The harvest is plenteous and the laborers are already too few. Therefore, we should spend all of our time involved in the work of ministry.

CHAPTER 11

Don't Worry, Be Happy!

Philippians 4:6–9

Anxious about Things
    The Problem with Worrying
    The Prescription for Worshipers
    The Peace from Worshiping
Addressing Our Thoughts
    Positive Thinking Builds Character
    Positive Thinking Breeds Cleanliness
    Positive Thinking Births Christians
Applying the Truth
    The Powerful Preaching
    The Perfect Practice
    The Promised Peace

Anxious about Things (4:6)

The Problem with Worrying (6a)

In Philippians 4:6a, Paul says, "Be careful for nothing. . . ." The New Testament equivalent of the word for worry means to be careful or anxious, or to take thought. The word "worry" comes from the Greek word *merimnao*, a combination of two words: *merizo*, which means "to divide," and *nous*, which means "mind." Therefore, worry means to have a mind divided between two outcomes—a possible negative one and a possible positive one. In Matthew 6:25, Jesus says, "Therefore I say unto you, Take no thought for your life, what ye shall eat, or what ye shall drink; nor yet for your body, what ye shall put on. . . ." Paul basically repeated the commandment of Jesus for us not to worry.

Worry is something produced by Satan. He loves for Christians to worry about things because he knows that it will prevent certain things from happening. Worry will do several things in the life of the believer. Worry will affect our *worship*. It is impossible to worry and worship at the same time. In order to worship God in spirit and in truth, we cannot allow our minds to be divided. Worry will affect our *witness*. When we worry, it becomes difficult to lead others to Christ. When people see our long faces, they would rather pass on receiving our Savior as their Savior.

Worry will affect our *work*. I normally work on Sunday's sermons on Tuesdays. One Tuesday, I was worried about a financial situation and I could not work on the sermon. The worrying affected my focus. Lastly, worry will affect our *wisdom*. Isn't it amazing how worry keeps you from remembering how God has brought you out of situations far worse than what you are presently facing?

The Prescription for Worshipers (6b)

Next, Paul says, ". . . But in every thing by prayer and supplication with thanksgiving let your requests be made known unto God" (4:6b). The prescription for worry is prayer and praise. The Lord is concerned about every detail in our lives. In 1 Thessalonians 5:16–18, Paul said, "Rejoice evermore. Pray without ceasing. In every thing give thanks: for this is the will of God in Christ Jesus concerning you." Prayer should be a continuous process in the life of the believer. When you pray about everything, you will pray without ceasing.

Prayer is more than communicating with God. Prayer means that we enter His presence. As we approach the throne of grace, there should be a spirit of praise and worship. This is the reason why Paul tells us to rejoice and be thankful when we pray. Prayer will cause our worries to cease. When we pray, we are not informing God of things He's unaware of. He knows all about our needs before we know them. He is just waiting to hear from His children. Instead of worrying, we should enter a time of worship through prayer.

The Peace from Worshiping (7)

As a result of worshiping God through prayer, Paul says, "And the peace of God, which surpasseth all understanding, shall keep your hearts and minds through Christ Jesus" (4:7). If the Lord is keeping your mind, you don't have to worry about it being divided. When we spend time worshiping God through prayer, we receive peace. The peace of God is awesome. When the Jews greeted each other, they wished each other peace by using the Hebrew term, *Shalom*. What a wonderful way to greet someone. They had peace on their minds at all times. It was a constant reminder of the peace of God that is available for all. In a real sense, they were speaking peace on each other. We should practice this when we greet our brothers and sisters in Christ. It would remind us that no matter what we encounter, the peace of God is available in that situation.

When we pray, we are praying to *Jehovah-shalom*, or "God, our peace." God desires to give us peace that is difficult to comprehend. When we see believers sick but smiling, it is due to God's peace. When a believer praises God after he or she has been unjustly terminated from a job, the peace of God is at work. The peace of God exists not only before the storm, it exists also during and beyond the storm. God desires to take your worrying and replace it with peace.

Addressing Our Thoughts (4:8)

Positive Thinking Builds Character (8a)

Paul says, "Finally, brethren, whatsoever things are true, whatsoever things are honest, whatsoever things are just . . ." (4:8a). Paul gives a list of things that produce character. First, Paul deals with *the honest thing to do*. Instead of focusing on the false things in life, we should focus or think about those things that are true. It is our knowledge of truth that liberates us. Our thoughts should always center on truth and honesty instead of on things that are false and deceptive.

Next, he deals with *the honorable thing to do*. The word Paul used here is *semnos*, which can be translated "honorable" or "noble." As believers, we must be people of nobility. We should not think crude or degrading thoughts at any time. Our thoughts should always be respectable and honorable. Next, he deals with *the harmless thing to do*. We should think about things that are just. We should make sure that our thoughts are righteous by both divine and human standards. This will cause us to be harmless to all people.

Positive Thinking Breeds Cleanliness (8b)

Paul gives a list of things that promote cleanliness: ". . . Whatsoever things are pure, whatsoever things are lovely, whatsoever things are of good report . . ." (4:8b). First, he deals with *godly* thoughts. Our thoughts should never become perverted or pornographic. Pure thoughts will lead to pure living. Next, he deals with *gracious* thoughts. Lovely thoughts are gracious and kind. When we read 1 Corinthians 13, we see how thinking these thoughts will lead to lovely living. Lastly, he deals with *good* thoughts. When others start talking about foolish and filthy things, we need to leave. If the talk is not good, listening to it can plant those kinds of thoughts in your mind. The next thing you know, you are telling that same nasty joke to someone else.

Positive Thinking Births Christians (8c)

Paul says, ". . . If there be any virtue, and if there be any praise, think on these things" (4:8c). You are not a Christian because you say it. You are a Christian because you live it. All of the things mentioned in this verse will lead to a virtuous life deserving of praise. Christianity is seen in our conduct. It all boils down to this basic fact: If you do not learn to take every thought captive to the obedience of Christ (2 Cor. 10:5b), your lifestyle will not be pleasing to the Lord. When we start thinking righteously, we will start acting that way. As we read the terms Paul used in Philippians 4:8, we see a beautiful description of Jesus Christ. When we begin to think like this, a beautiful image of Jesus will be projected through our lives.

Applying the Truth (4:9)

The Powerful Preaching (9a)

In Philippians 4:9a, Paul says, "Those things, which you have both learned, and received, and heard, and seen in me. . . ." Paul was one of God's most powerful and profound preachers and teachers of all times. Paul had demonstrated what it really meant to be a soldier in the Lord's army. Paul viewed his life as a sermon. The Philippians and others had heard and seen some powerful sermons preached by this brother. He lived what he preached. It really adds power to the message when the messenger is an example of what he preaches. The word that people received about Paul was that when he was absent from them, he acted the same as when he was present. When someone came from Ephesus or Corinth after being with Paul, the Philippians were told that he was acting just as holy there as he had when in their presence. His life in the pulpit matched his living in every other place.

It is hard to listen to a person teach or preach about the danger of intoxicating drink when he is standing before you drunk. Our way of living speaks volumes before we ever open our mouths. When we can use our lives as examples for others it pleases our Father in heaven.

The Perfect Practice (9b)

He told them to "do" (4:9b) what they had seen him do and to abide by the truth they had learned from him. In other words, if they wanted to be faithful, they needed to behave faithfully. Practice does not make perfect. Perfect practice makes perfect. They had seen it and now they could do it. God had blessed them by giving them one of the greatest models the world had to offer. Now they needed to start imitating him in the same way he imitated Christ. It didn't matter how much they had heard or seen if they did not apply it to their lives.

I can prepare the spiritual meal and serve it, but I cannot make anyone eat it. God does not allow me to force feed His Word to others. All I can do is preach it from my lips and from my life. It is up to the believers to apply it.

The Promised Peace (9c)

Paul says, ". . . And the God of peace shall be with you" (4:9c). Once again, we are told that the peace of God will be there for us if we live according to the Word. Paul wanted the saints to know that God's peace was available for them. All of the things Paul mentioned in this section were shared so they could obtain the peace of God. If their thoughts were right, their actions would be right. Proper thoughts and actions will lead to God's peace. Isaiah 26:3 says, "Thou wilt keep him in perfect peace, whose mind is stayed on thee: because he trusteth in thee."

CHAPTER 12

Contentment in Christ

Philippians 4:10–23

The Satisfied Soldier
    The Appreciation for the Package
    The Attitude of the Prisoner
    The Application of the Principle
The Shared Substance
    The Reason for His Satisfaction
    The Reliance on Their Substance
    The Reward for Their Spirit
The Savior's Supply
    The Sufficient Supply
    The Sweet-smelling Sacrifice
    The Superintendent's Storehouse
    The Special Salutations

The Satisfied Soldier (4:10–12)

The Appreciation for the Package (10)

In Philippians 4:10, Paul says, "But I rejoiced in the Lord greatly, that now at the last your care of me hath flourished again; wherein ye were also careful, but ye lacked opportunity." The Philippians had sent Paul a financial gift. That apparently was not the first time that had happened because Paul said, "it flourished [or blossomed] again." In this letter, Paul repeatedly shared how much he loved those saints in Philippi. Their sending a financial gift to him made it evident that they loved him as well. Love is an action word. If love is stated and never shown, it probably does not exist. Paul did not take their gifts for granted. He didn't just send a little thank-you note. He wrote a long letter to express his gratitude. We should always be thankful when someone does something nice for us. There is nothing more despicable than sharing your substance with someone and not hearing the words "thank you." Paul wanted to let his friends know how grateful he was for the love they continued to demonstrate. Paul rejoiced in the Lord for their generosity. By the way, we should always give the Lord some praise when others do nice things for us. If it weren't for God stirring the hearts of men, those nice things would not take place. God is the one who initiates the thoughts of kindness that lead to the deeds of men.

In Philippians 4:10, Paul was not complaining when he said, ". . . That now at the last. . . ." When we examine the verse, it sounds like Paul was saying, "It's about time!" This is not the case at all. Paul knew how difficult it was for the saints to get this gift to him. They did not have the services of Western Union or Fed Ex to get the gift to Paul. They desired to send the gift long before it arrived, but they lacked the opportunity to do so. Although the Roman roads were impressive during this period in history, the Philippians probably had difficulty finding someone to deliver this gift to Paul for them. Any affiliation with a person in prison was dangerous. Many probably shied away out of fear if they were asked to deliver the gift. The day finally came when they were able to send one of their own, Epaphroditus, with the gift.

The Attitude of the Prisoner (11)

In Philippians 4:11, Paul says, "Not that I speak in respect of want. . . ." The Greek word translated want is *husteresis*, which means "destitution." Paul wanted the saints to know he was grateful for their gift. He considered it a blessing when it arrived. On the other hand, he wanted them to know that he was not down to his last dime either. He was not speaking to them from a state of destitution. He wasn't trying to get more from them. He simply wanted his friends to know that there was contentment before the gift arrived as well as after it arrived.

Paul had made it to a state of spiritual growth that is amazing to most of us. He says, ". . . For I have learned, in whatsoever state I am, therewith to be content" (4:11b). Dissatisfaction is a basic human condition. Everyone desires to be satisfied in life. However, for most of us, the circumstances and conditions of life determine whether or not we will be satisfied. This was not the case for Paul. He was satisfied whether he was a *chained prisoner* or a *church planter.* He was satisfied with money or without money. In other words, Paul had learned to live above the circumstances and conditions of life.

The Application of the Principle (12)

He says, "I know both how to be abased, and I know how to abound: every where and in all things I am instructed both to be full and to be hungry, both to abound and to suffer need" (4:12). The word "abound" means "more than enough." The word "abased" means "to run low." When these words are used, the image of a fuel tank gauge comes to mind. On one end of the gauge, there is the letter "F" for full and on the other end is the letter "E" for empty. Paul wanted his friends to know that no matter where the arrow pointed, he had learned to be satisfied.

If we were honest, most of us would have to admit that we haven't made it to this point. We may quote this passage when we have a lot of things working in our favor. Oh, it isn't hard to recite Philippians 4:11–12, when you have a nice job, a big house and two or three cars in the garage. It's not hard when the bills have been paid, the doctor gives a good report, and the family is doing fine. What happens when the circumstances of life change on you? What happens when you stop abounding and find yourself abased? It is easy to write something like this from a penthouse, but Paul is writing it from prison. At any time, Paul could possibly be sentenced to death, yet he is satisfied. Paul had learned to depend totally on God. The word "instructed" in Philippians 4:12 comes from the Greek word *musterion,* which means "I have learned the secret or mystery." He had learned the secret of enjoying contentment with or without food.

The Shared Substance (4:13–17)

The Reason for His Satisfaction (13)

How was Paul able to be contented over and above his circumstances? Well, the answer is found in the most familiar verse that most of us can quote from the letter to the Philippians. Paul says, "I can do all things through Christ which strengtheneth me" (4:13). In this letter to the Philippians, we have learned about Paul's commitment, courage, comfort, confidence, and contentment. All of these Christian characteristics could be seen in the prisoner's life. He was able to do these things by relying on a power greater than his own.

The Greek word *endunamoo* is translated "strengtheneth." Paul was able to do all things through the power of Jesus Christ. 1 John 4:4 says, "Ye are of God, little children, and have overcome them: because greater is he that is in you, than he that is in the world." From the beginning of his Christian life, Paul had been strengthened by Jesus Christ. In Acts 9, we read about Paul's conversion. After Paul gave his life to Christ, the Bible says, "But Saul increased the more in strength . . ." (Acts 9:22). When we give our lives to Christ and become committed to ministry, He will allow us to increase in strength.

When serving the Savior leads to suffering, we will always be given the strength to endure. Jesus equipped Paul with power to deal with everything that he needed to in order to accomplish His will. On one occasion, Paul's involvement in ministry led to a storm. While traveling to Rome, the ship was lost at sea after encountering a serious storm. All of the people on board—crew and passengers—feared for their lives. They had lost all hope. There was one on the ship who still had hope. Paul stood up and said, "And now I exhort you to be of good cheer: for there shall be no loss of any man's life among you, but of the ship. For there stood by me this night the angel of God, whose I am, and whom I serve" (Acts 27:22–23). Paul's satisfaction was based on his strength through the Savior.

The Reliance on Their Substance (14–16)

Paul had been in dire financial need before, and the Philippians had been there to help him. When Paul first started on his missionary journey, he divided his time between spiritual work and secular work. As he traveled, he would use his tent-making skills to earn an income. When the work of evangelism flourished, he had to discontinue the secular work to concentrate totally on the spiritual work. There were days he went without nutritional supplement for the sake of ministry.

In the beginning, the other churches planted by Paul did not do what the Philippians did on a regular basis. It appears that other churches started assisting Paul by the time he started his third missionary journey. The church at Philippi seemingly had included Paul in their church budget from the beginning. They wanted to support the work that he was doing all over the region. They could not accompany him on those trips, but they could assist him. His friends at Philippi had come through for him on many occasions, and it was always on time. The gifts from them came during his affliction, and he was appreciative.

The Reward for Their Spirit (17)

Paul says, "Not because I desire a gift: but I desire fruit that may abound to your account" (4:17). Paul was not trying to get more from the Philippians. He was not trying to butter them up in order to receive additional assistance. There are times when people say nice things to you only to try and get something from you. Paul made it clear to the saints that this was not the case for him. Paul was not out to rob the saints and fill his belly like those he talked about in Philippians 3:19. He loved the saints at Philippi and appreciated their generosity.

I had an associate who invited me to share during his church's clergy appreciation services. I participated for three years. The first year I preached in February. The second year, I preached in August. The third year, I preached in April. On the last occasion, I asked him, "Why do you have me to come at different times during the year to preach during your appreciation service?"

He said, "Karry, you just preach at one of my appreciation services. I have twelve services each year." Not only was that the last time I participated in the celebration, it wasn't too much later that the people in the church decided to discontinue these monthly celebrations that drained them of their resources. The preacher decided to leave the church since they wanted to have a clergy appreciation service for him annually rather than monthly.

Paul desired "fruit that [would] abound to [their] account" (4:17b). In other words, their giving to Paul meant that they supported the work of Paul that had been ordained from above. Therefore, their contributions were being recorded above. They were laying up treasures in heaven. Their heavenly "blessing account" was running over.

The Savior's Supply (4:18–23)

The Sufficient Supply (18a)

The words written by Paul in the next verse prove that Paul was not fishing for additional funds. He said, ". . . I have all, and abound: I am full, having received of Epaphroditus the things which were sent from you. . ." (4:18a). His cup and cupboard were running over as a result of their gift. In essence, he was saying that he now had all that he needed as a result of receiving their gift. They had not sent just a financial blessing to Paul; they had sent "things" to him.

While growing up in Arkansas, I spent time with my grandfather who was a pastor of two small churches in different towns. Most of the members of these congregations were farmers and did not have much money. I remember that when my grandfather made it home on Sunday evenings, we would go and unload the trunk of his car. All of the things we pulled out of the trunk had been given to him by members of those congregations. Someone may have butchered a pig and given Papa one of the hams. Someone else gave him eggs from the hen house. Someone else had churned some butter and gave Papa a bowl of it. Another may have shared some of the tomatoes and peas from the garden or fruit from the tree. I'll put it this way: We never went hungry.

The Sweet-smelling Sacrifice (18b)

In describing the gift, Paul says, ". . . an odour of a sweet smell, a sacrifice acceptable, wellpleasing to God" (4:18b). Paul compared the gift from the Philippians to the offerings of the Old Testament. In chapters 1–3 of Leviticus, there are three special offerings labeled as sweet-savor offerings: the burnt offering, the meal offering, and the peace offering. All three of these offerings delighted the heart of God. Paul wanted the Philippians to know that their generous gift was like those offerings. Not only was he pleased, God was well-pleased as well. He wanted them to realize that they pleased God with their efforts. Their support of his ministry was like a lovely fragrance flowing into the nostrils of God.

There are a couple of national and international ministries that I support. I realize that the ministers associated with these ministries are being blessed by what I send, but I am not doing it just for them. I recognize the spiritual worth of their ministries and the number of souls that are being reached by their efforts and publications. My main goal is to please God as these ministers please God with their efforts.

The Superintendent's Storehouse (19–20)

When Paul thought about the sacrificial gift from the saints, he immediately thought about God's sufficient storehouse to supply all of their needs. He says, ". . . My God shall supply all your need according to his riches in glory by Christ Jesus" (4:19). In this chapter, Paul revealed so many benefits made available through Christ Jesus. Earlier, he spoke of the *peace of God* made available through Christ (v. 7). Next, he spoke of the *power of God* made available through Christ (v. 13). Here in verse 19, he talks about the *provisions of God* made available through Him.

When Paul mentioned their sacrifice in verse 18, he compared their gift to the Old Testament offerings as well as informing us of the financial status of the saints. The Philippian saints were not wealthy. They probably had to dig deep to send this gift to Paul and pay Epaphroditus' fare to deliver it. It really was a sacrificial gift. Paul wanted them to know that God was going to take care of them by supplying for all of their needs. All they needed was available through Christ from the Father's storehouse. The Philippians obviously understood the principle of giving outlined in Luke 6:38: "Give, and it shall be given unto you; good measure, pressed down, and shaken together, and running over, shall men give unto your bosom. For with the same measure that ye mete withal it shall be measured to you again." I am a living witness that it works.

After he thought about God's storehouse, a doxology flowed from his pen. He says, "Now unto God and our Father be glory for ever and ever. Amen". (4:20). When he thought about God supplying their needs, he immediately gave the doxology and said, "Amen!" What else is left for a person to say other than, "Amen, Amen, Amen"?

The Special Salutations (21–23)

He closed the letter by saying, "Salute every saint in Christ Jesus" (4:21a). In other words, "Tell all of my brothers and sisters in Christ that I said, 'hello.'"

Just before putting his pen down, Paul gave his last words. First, we have the *courageous comrades* (4:21b) in Rome mentioned. Timothy and others wanted Paul to tell the Philippians "hello" for them. Next, he deals with the *Christian congregations* (4:22) in Rome. There were some saints in Rome. Many of them had become converts since Paul's imprisonment. The saints in Caesar's household had probably been led to Christ by Paul while he was under house arrest. Finally, we have the *concluding comments* (4:23) from Rome. Paul gave the benediction: "The grace of our Lord Jesus Christ be with you all. Amen" (4:23). The letter opens with grace (1:2) and closes with grace (4:23). Everything that Paul wrote in this letter is sandwiched between grace. Amen!

To order additional copies of

REJOICING IN THE LORD

Have your credit card ready and call

toll free (877) 421-READ (7323)

or send $12.99* each plus $4.95 S&H**

to

WinePress Publishing
PO Box 428
Enumclaw, WA 98022
www.winepresspub.com

or

Antioch Fellowship Church
7550 S. Hampton Rd.
Dallas, TX 75232

*WA residents, add 8.4% sales tax

** Add $1.00 S&H for each additional book ordered.